[handwritten inscription:] Billy — Enjoy and Remember [...] from [signature] nov 202

Wonders and Miracles

EXPERIENCES, LESSONS AND SIGNS FROM ABOVE
ENCOUNTERED DURING MY EARTHLY JOURNEY

Wonders and Miracles

EXPERIENCES, LESSONS AND SIGNS FROM ABOVE
ENCOUNTERED DURING MY EARTHLY JOURNEY

N. B. JOHNSON

Accomplishing
Innovation Press

Library of Congress Control Number: 2022932803

Paperback ISBN-13: 978-1-64450-555-7
Audiobook ISBN-13: 978-1-64450-553-3
Ebook ISBN-13: 978-1-64450-554-0

ACKNOWLEDGEMENTS

I'd like to thank my family. Their love, laughter and encouragement as observers and occasionally participants along my journey were greatly appreciated and accepted. Imagine living with, being married to, and a close relative of someone like me. There were many 'Aha' moments.

Thanks to Gloria Bekoe, an earthly mentor and guide, for her wisdom and encouragement. And to Harriet Leff, who literally found and coaxed me into using healing hands on people other than family. She also introduced me to a meditation retreat community that led to enhanced spiritual growth and development. I came into contact with several people at the retreat who literally changed my life. It was a blessing to receive the guidance of Orest Bedrij, a gifted author whose amazing aura is filled with light and love. William (*Bill*) Hungerford and Nancy Bragin exposed all attendees to a spiritually based method for raising consciousness levels.

Harvey Johnson, my Consultant, encouraged me to write about my experiences. He read my initial version and the revised ones, questioning and scribbling comments where he felt additional clarification was needed.

Finally, I'd like to offer sincere gratitude to my agent Deidre Johnson for her expertise. She took my quite inexperienced initial offering, and through editorial advising, patiently directed me into producing a manuscript worthy of being published.

Thank you to my editorial team: Deidre Johnson, Angela Campbell (*Ph.D.*) and Valerie Willis (a *gifted author*). Without their continuous persistence, guidance and patience this publication would not have been possible.

TABLE OF CONTENTS

PART 1

PART 2

PART 3

APPENDICES

PREFACE

I've been asked many times about things and events encountered during this life's journey on Planet Earth. Family and friends encouraged me to put them into writing. They mentioned other relatives might have been involved in some of the same occurrences but were hesitant to voice them. So, here are some of my adventurous wonders and miracles. Included are also thoughts and beliefs, some born with and others acquired along the way.

All of the episodes in this book happened; however, I've changed names to protect the privacy of individuals involved.

Someone said we are spiritual beings having a physical experience on Planet Earth. I view this place as a school where we come to learn. From my point of view, there are no right or wrong things, good or bad events, or mistakes. There are only challenges and lessons to assist in gaining knowledge. They offer an opportunity for us to evolve to different levels of understanding and consciousness. After reading, digesting the information and trying to sort through the pros and cons, I've come to understand that God is love. I don't accept the Old Testament view showing Him as vengeful and punishing. My belief is that God, Divine Source, or Universal Creator is responsible for all that was, is now and yet to come.

Everything on Planet Earth including the Planet itself vibrates. Using Dr. David Hawkins Scale of Human Consciousness, we can calibrate a numerical reference for the frequency. Heaviness yields a low number. Light hearted ranks at a higher number.

During our journey, enticements will come in the form of the seven deadly sins found in the Holy Bible: greed, wrath, lust, sloth, pride, envy and gluttony. The accompanying behaviors we exhibit if we are thus enticed are: shame, guilt, apathy, grief, fear, hatred and anger. They tend to make us feel heavy hearted.

We will be exposed to many situations offering us growth and development. You might have heard people express feeling heavy hearted or weighed down by events in their lives. Or perhaps the person might have said he/she felt like walking on air. The more experiences we have and master, the greater our growth in consciousness and the lighter our bodies seem.

When we're to learn a lesson, other people can be involved. But, they're only bystanders to assist us. The lesson is ours alone. The important thing is not the problem, but how we handle it. It's all about us and no one else. This concept is important to understand. Everyone has his/her own personal journey but you might on occasion be called upon to help someone else during their struggle.

Divine Source gave us free will to make choices. Sometimes we like to blame others for the decisions we made. It's necessary to acknowledge that's simply an excuse to do what we wanted but not accept responsibility for the outcome. If this sojourn on Planet Earth is for our growth and development, then we have to realize that the only person who can change an individual's behavior is the person him or herself.

When experiencing a lesson, handle the situation from a truth perspective. Give it your best shot and no matter what the outcome you will have peace of mind. It's nice to be able to look at your reflection in the mirror with a clear conscience. When you speak from truth, the Universe has your back. If there are so-called repercussions, they will only come because Divine Source is using the wisdom gained from participating for your further enlightenment.

Stay true to yourself. Know that whatever fate or destiny has planned for you will occur. And nothing you say or do will alter the Universe's ultimate plan. If you don't accomplish your goal in this lifetime, you will come back. So, relax and humbly surrender to your journey in this lifetime.

INTRODUCTION

Planet Earth is currently moving from the Age of Pisces to the Age of Aquarius. Pisces was domination by hierarchy and power. Religion, political ideology and charismatic leaders guided people's lives. It was the age of secrets hidden in caves, temples and behind closed doors. Many religions flourished. It's zodiac symbol of a fish was used to represent Jesus and Christianity.

Aquarius is the age of information. With the onset of the computer and internet, events are instantly shared around the world. When the Dali Lama and his Monks fled Tibet, they exposed Western societies to many Eastern Practices that had been sheltered in monasteries. During the past fifty years, self-awareness, meditation, and alternative healing have emerged.

A constant refrain among people is: Why Am I Here? What is my purpose? Subconsciously we know we've come to Planet Earth to personally participate in learning something. We just don't remember what.

What if we've all come to Earth at this time to experience the cosmic shift as we move from the familiar to the unknown? A worldwide pandemic and climate change are part of this. It's our choice whether to accept the onset of new ideas and ways of life to the demise of old habits and practices. Change is upon us. It will happen whether we want it to or not.

My belief is we are pre-programmed to gain certain knowledge. We don't have to look for the lessons, they will find us. Our purpose for being here during this symbolic cosmic shift is to have a wealth of experiences and to learn from them. Various situations and events are already designed to assist our growth in consciousness.

Although we don't all look alike, we are part of one family, the Human Race. Everyone's basic physical structure is made up of the same components. What alters is the costumes we put on and our resistance or acceptance of our purpose for being here.

I've been looking at my life and wondering what's it all about. What's the purpose of my existence here on this planet at this time? As I look around I see death, destruction and despair. Yet, I also see the multiple positive changes that have occurred in our country and around the world.

The last several years have seen our civilization go from a computer that took up an entire city block to one that fits into the palm of a hand. From newspapers that took days and weeks for information to become known, to social media distributing news instantaneously around the globe. Cardboard and aluminum robots of the past have evolved to ones with artificial intelligence that learn as they're utilized. After flying into the upper atmosphere and out of Earth's gravitational tug, astronauts can now live in space. Planetary probes soar past our moon to visit asteroids and outer galactic destinations.

With great technological advances, we've strayed from a healthy respect for nature and ourselves to constant bombardment of both light and noise. Daily, we witness the slow destruction of our planet through waste of natural resources and a glut of trash circling our planet, defiling our oceans and poisoning the waterways. Some species have also become extinct.

Why are we here? Who knows. But I believe that in our Universe things happen the way they're supposed to and all is as it should be. Thy Will Be Done.

Part 1

Chapter 1

Astral Travel

The astral world, after all, is like a doorway between the
physical world and the higher dimensions.

Tana Hoy

We have several bodies. Everyone is accustomed to our physical form. It is what's visible when looking into a mirror; the figure we can feed and clothe. Some people are also aware of a second body, the Etheric one. This is a duplicate of our physical frame located about an inch or two away from it. It's the means by which the mind and soul are able to make contact with the physical body. We can't see it, but we can feel or sense it on occasion.

When someone loses a body part due to illness, accident or war an interesting thing can occur. The arm, leg or finger is no longer in our three-dimensional viewed realm. But, it still exists as part of our etheric shape. We can feel pain sensation in the missing arm or leg even though we can't see it. In medical terms this is known as Phantom Limb Sensation.

Anyone who has suffered the loss of a leg can still have pain in that area. It feels like it's still attached but injured. In the energy medicine course I took, we were told to treat the missing part as if it's still there to help ease healing.

When we astral travel, our two bodies are attached by an etheric cord. This is our personal guidance system. It ensures that we always return to our physical self and not float off into space. *Ecclesiastes Chapter 12 in the Bible, mentions this silver cord.*

Astral travel can occur anytime we go into a relaxed state of rest. During this deep sleep, the etheric body can remove itself from the physical one and float into space. It's not a total detachment because there's a life line linking them together. At the end of travel time, this cord guides the etheric body back so it can reattach to its physical form.

Many of us are unaware of the night sight seeing we do. Usually, it's an easy detachment and return. Sometimes, we are more alert to something having happened. Have you ever suddenly jerked awake during the night? If you have, you might have been experiencing a rough reconnection. It's like an airplane landing. Most of the time flight landings are easy and peaceful. Every once is a while, a plane might have a rough one due to an air current or pilot misjudging. Jerking awake lets us know our wandering body was just reattaching itself.

Lots of people keep a water bottle next to their bed. Sometimes during the night, they wake up really dry mouth and need to take a sip of water before returning to sleep. When you astral travel, often times you will return thirsty and need that sip of water. Usually you go right back to sleep.

Problem Solving

Have you ever had a situation you couldn't solve? Perhaps it's still on your mind when you go to bed. The next morning, you wake up knowing the solution. It's as if you went to class during the night and someone showed you how to solve the problem.

> *Memory comes of the time I was making a combination bedspread with matching window decor for our bedroom. The drapes were easy to construct but, there was a bit of difficulty with the bed covering. I wanted a professional look and the corners were not falling the way they should. After several frustrating attempts, I quit. But of course those corners were on my mind when falling asleep that night. Upon awakening the next morning, I knew exactly what to do and finished the bedspread in no time. It's as if I'd gone to a sewing session during the night and learned what to do.*

Night travel after going to bed is a natural part of life. If you think back, you might recall a time when you went to sleep worried and woke up the next morning feeling at peace. Or, when you fell asleep with a problem you found unsolvable and woke up the next morning knowing the solution.

OBE (Out of Body Experiences)

People involved in life and death trauma often talk about having 'Out of Body' experiences. When this occurs, they usually describe leaving their body on the ground (*in case of an accident*) or on the operating table (*in case of medical surgery*), only to find themselves floating above their physical form watching everything that happens. Eventually, they will consciously return to their physique and awaken back to this earthly existence.

When this occurs, one of your bodies floats into space, but is still attached to the other by the etheric cord. Once the decision is made not to transition, but to return to life, it uses this attachment to return to it's rightful place.

Traveling Episodes

I've always loved looking at the sky, finding it very peaceful and calming. Seeing the different levels of clouds as a child made it fun to imagine animals in their shapes. From sunrise to sunset you can view a kaleidoscope of colors depending on the weather patterns. At night I still enjoy looking at the heavens, but with the cloudy conditions and a light cap from being close to the city, it's almost impossible to see the star patterns now. Recently, I've become aware of a very bright small light that never seems to move. It's visible during the night and at dawn in the sky. I'm not sure if it's a satellite or a planet.

Having a tendency to travel when falling asleep is so relaxing. Soaring high in the air it's soothing to look down over hills and valleys with luscious landscape. Flowers viewed from up above display an assortment of the most beautiful bright colors and leaves on trees are vivid shades of a variety of green. The air is clear and bright offering a sense of peace.

3

Lots of times I visit a vast water world. It's like being in the middle of the ocean with only calm peaceful undulating water extending in all directions.

My earliest astral travel recollection was when I visited my son. He had just started college away from home and I was a bit anxious. As a concerned parent, I needed to make sure he was okay. So, one night I went to visit. Looking into his dorm room I could see he was asleep and so was his roommate. After that visit, I felt quite relieved. I knew from my astral visit to him that he was fine. I never visited him at night again.

Astral projection can occur anytime for me. When necessary, I'll fall asleep and travel to do whatever needs to be done. This can be in the afternoon, early evenings or at night, often returning thirsty and immediately drinking water. Sometimes my travels are remembered and at other times it's as if I entered a black hole or void and have no recall.

My niece called one day to say that I visited her bedroom the night before. She had been ill and drifting in and out of sleep. She said I morphed through a wall. Seeing me calmed her down and she had a peaceful night sleep.

Occasionally, if there's a rough landing back into my physical body it'll jerk me awake. Most often, people travel as an observer high above the ground getting a bird's eye view of the landscape. They see a wealth of the most beautiful colors. Soaring over the Earth brings them peace and contentment. Sometimes when they awaken suddenly, they'll recall what they saw. Astral travel is just a part of our normal everyday Planet Earth experiences. But, one has to admit it's fascinating that humans are capable of so many adventures.

Chapter 2

TOOTS

Gone but never forgotten.

As a young girl, family members told me I was born with a veil over my face. That's an old wives' tale that meant a person was born blessed with certain abilities. I didn't really understand what that meant during my younger years and paid it no attention. Apparently, the elders thought there was something special about me.

My Mother was gifted, but I didn't realize it until later in life. She would have talks with me in the evening when my sisters were in bed or at another activity. Our conversations would be about situations in life that might have occurred in the past or events that may show up in the future. Her talks always included types of behavior to avoid. I had a temper and would defend myself and my property. "Never get angry," she would say. If you got mad, you lost the fight. (*I now understand that to mean displaying anger gives your power to the other person.*) You catch more flies with honey than vinegar was her way of encouraging me to be kind to others.

Belief in the Universal Law of Attraction. We attract to us what comes from within us. Expect the best and the best will come.

She would tell me to always share with my siblings because there's plenty more where that came from. This was a source of amusement since we were poor and didn't have a lot. But thinking back to the old days, I realized we never went hungry. There was always food on the table, a place to live, and money to purchase whatever necessities were needed. Meals as well as shelter was also available to friends or relatives who needed it. Whatever we had was shared with all.

Although she was my Mother, as a teenager, I renamed her "Toots". I didn't know anyone with that name and still have no idea where it came from. For me, it was an endearing affectionate title for a wonderful parent, mentor and friend full of kindness, goodness and generosity. Toots had an unshakeable faith in God and Jesus. She always said Jesus would provide for all of her needs.

> *The Law of Transmutation of Energy. Every thought we send has the power to choose positive or negative form.*

Toots preached kindness and forgiveness. Throughout her lifetime, I never heard her express an unpleasant thought or derogatory word about anyone. Her outlook involved always looking for the good in others. In every misfortune she believed there was a silver lining. As an optimist, she encouraged everyone to see the bright side of everything. One's thoughtful vibrations not only affect that person, but they also affect people around us. Sending unhappy thoughts created negative energy so Toots always sent blessings generating positive vibes. She was an amazing woman who was sincerely missed her when she transitioned.

Chapter 3

A Reason, A Season, A Lifetime

*Life is like a book. Some persons are there for a page,
some are there for a chapter, but true ones are there
throughout the whole story.*

FB–The Power Within You

Everyone has their own personal journey to walk in the Earth School. Occasionally when an event takes place, we don't always know whether the incident is for us or for someone else. In the intervening process, we can become an Earth Angel assisting another individual on their life path.

Job Assistance

Annette was working in an occupation that paid the bills, but wasn't quite sure about what she wanted to do. She often talked to family about finding a new position.

Roxanne, her cousin, was employed full time but decided to also work for a tax preparation firm in the evenings to earn an extra bit of cash. At this side job, she became friendly with one of the other accountants. In the process of talking, the young lady mentioned that her firm was hiring. After getting all the pertinent information from her co-worker, Roxanne called Annette and suggested she look into this new opportunity. With prospects for a higher paying job, her cousin followed through. She contacted the business and arranged an interview. Her meeting with the recruiters was successfully accomplished. Annette was offered a position with the firm.

The company had announced paying a bonus to any employee recommending someone for the open positions if that person was hired. This meant the young lady who worked at the company would be eligible to collect several thousand dollars since the person she recommended was now on payroll. Roxanne only worked at the tax preparation firm for a couple of months. She quit when her cousin got hired in the new occupation. The young lady who assisted in this process left both the tax firm and her other job too.

It's funny how things work. They say there are no coincidences. Thanks to this Universal intervention, Annette was placed in a position where she was pleasantly employed and making a comfortable salary. Roxanne and her co-worker met at a side job which they both left after just a few weeks. But, they were responsible for Annette's future career movement. They came together for a reason.

9/11 EVENT

Both of these young people were involved in the 9/11 events. Joselyn in Manhattan and her brother at the Pentagon.

Joselyn had been employed at a firm in Pennsylvania. One day she had a conversation with a fellow co-worker who expressed a desire to switch companies so he could live in Bermuda. She thought this was a great idea and decided to change companies too. It would be exciting to work in Manhattan. Her new job began April 11th, a block from the New York City World Trade Center complex.

Paul was a member of the military. His position at that time was working at the Pentagon. On that fateful day when the news media announced that an airplane had hit the World Trade Center in New York City, he was immediately concerned. His sister got off the train at that station going to work. Wanting to find out more information about what was occurring, he left the office in search of a television.

While away from the desk, the Pentagon like the World Trade Center buildings, was targeted for destruction. The crash impact and resultant fire ball instantly killed everyone in his office. There was also widespread burning of victims and massive destruction to the Pentagon.

Joselyn started working in Manhattan on 4/11. The destruction to both the World Trade Center Complex and the Pentagon occurred five months later on 9/11. Her brother's life was spared because he went looking for news about his sister. Had she still been working in Pennsylvania, he might have been one of the fatalities.

New York City was just a short blip on her employment schedule. Within a year she was living and working in another state. Things happen the way they are supposed to. Divine Source protected both of them.

People come into our lives for a reason, a season, a lifetime. And, there are no coincidences. There's a lot to consider. For the brother and sister, it wasn't their time to transition. They both have a further purpose here in the Earth School. Time will let them both know what it is.

VISION ENCOUNTER

My dreams usually flow like a movie from one scene to another. This was no dream. The individual was still there like a photograph. Only the head and shoulders of a female was visible. She was dressed in an African garb with a band of the same material covering her hair.

I saw her as a silhouette side view, not a frontal one. The vision remained long enough to be imprinted into my mind's eye. Even now after all these years while it's not as vivid, I can still recall it to memory.

When I awakened, I wondered about her. This was someone I didn't know. The question became who was she and why did she appear to me? Instantly, the thought comes to mind that she's my spiritual advisor. The impression was of a peaceful person so there was no fear, only curiosity.

A couple of weeks after this occurred, I went on a weekend retreat with a bus load of people, mostly women. Once we checked into our hotel, four of us grouped together to travel around during this visit. One of ladies, Giselle, was a stranger I'd never met. The first day we enjoyed seeing a play and having dinner together. That evening relaxing with Giselle and both of our roommate in her hotel suite, we conversed about life. It was a really enjoyable evening.

The next day after breakfast the four of us went shopping at a local mall. We had lunch together then went to our respective rooms to rest before dinner. A banquet meal was planned for everyone who came with us on the tour. Giselle was seated at the table next to me and my roommate. When she turned her head in profile, I was stunned. This was the woman I had seen in my vision almost two weeks before. We had been socializing together for two days. Yet, I didn't recognize her until she wore the same African attire and sat with the exact silhouette profile pose. My vision had now come to life.

Later that evening I told Giselle about seeing her in a dream, but not recognizing her until she wore the African dress and head scarf. Interesting enough, she explained that she had put on another outfit and at the last minute felt the need to change into what she was now wearing.

We chatted at length that evening and on the bus trip back home. She was a font of wisdom. I talked with her about some of my concerns. Without hesitation, she took the time to help me work through them for answers. Her advice helped to prepare me for experiences that would come up over the next several years. She was always only a telephone call away.

There's a saying that when the pupil is ready the teacher will appear. Giselle was a true spiritual advisor who came into my life for a reason and a season.

Chapter 4

ILLUSION

All the world's a stage, and all of the men and women merely players…

William Shakespeare

- Illusion: An object only has the reality we give it.
- Illusionist: A self-conceited person who uses words to boost his ego.
- Illusionists: People looking for a dream.

According to the book *A Course in Miracles*, everything is an illusion. Our minds create what we see, how we feel about things, and gives them their meaning. Should this be true, then everyone is really participating in the same dream.

We are all One. If life is an illusion and a creation of the mind or ego, then we must all be connected or inter-connected. One family with members of different colors, genders and religious preferences. My relatives, individually and collectively must all be having the same dream as me. In fact, the entire Planet Earth's population has to be a part of the entire fabric of our illusion.

How we individually react to being in this earthly dream reflects different states of consciousness. Some of us respond emotionally to almost every stimuli or event that occurs. We behave with our most base emotions of anger, jealousy and hate. Others respond with love, compassion and forgiveness.

Many people can see and hear the same spoken words but process them differently. In the Bible's 'Sowing of Seeds' parable, found in the Gospel of St. Matthew, it tells us that words are like seeds that fall on the ground. They can become powerful if they fall on fertile ears or they can lose all of their energy if they land on barren ears.

Oneness of humanity is certainly recognized by the multiple acts of Mother Nature. The weather affects everyone regardless of size, shape, race, gender and economic level. When it rains, snows or floods it doesn't discriminate. Earthquakes, wildfires and volcanic eruptions occur throughout the world.

In medical practice on a global level, Oneness is also recognized. When a person is cut, he/she will bleed red blood. When tragedies happen blood transfusions are administered worldwide. People in need of an organ donor will accept the first one available regardless of nationality or gender. Our bodies and souls are indeed One with each other.

William Shakespeare wrote in his play _As You Like It_, "Are we all illusionists taking part in the same dream?" When we accept the illusion we are One, peace and harmony will have a chance to reign supreme.

Chapter 5

VIBRATION / CALIBRATION / ENERGY

Energy cannot be created or destroyed. It can only be
mastered, directed, and transformed.

Norma Milanovich & Shirley McCune

Humans are a combination of energy, liquid and mass with skeletal bones to give shape and a vessel made out of skin to hold it all together in a form called the body. Within this physique I believe we have a God spark called the soul. This life force controls all of the contents within the body, giving it the ability to feel emotions, to learn based on experiences and the capacity to move and function.

Each animate and inanimate object in this earthly environment, has its own frequency code. Everything energetically vibrates. Our bodies vibrating rates can fluctuate reflecting our current state of mind. When we're weighed down with apathy or shame, our body feels heavy. If we're filled with anger, hatred, and feelings of negativity, we can feel emotionally weighed down and our vibration frequency or calibration level is at a lower score.

When we have peace, joy and love within us we feel light as if walking on air. Our calibration level numbers will be higher. It's not the conditions we live in or under that determine our personal calibration level, but how we co-exist or react to these situations.

Our vocabulary, the words we use, can often explain how we feel. For instance, when we're sad, we say we are heavy hearted. At happy and joyful occasions, we say we're light hearted. When angry, our words indicate we're filled with rage or mad. Worries weigh us down, etc. We instinctively know whether we're registering light or heavy. *This energetic component of our body can be measured using Dr. David Hawkins 'Scale of Human Consciousness' found in his book Letting Go.* He believed Energy followed thought. What's within us consciously is manifested and can be calibrated.

Our family resided in a twin house located in a semi-rural neighborhood. We grew vegetables and occasionally raised chickens in the back yard. My Mother *(Toots)* was great for having us bless our food and thank God for all that we had. She said you could be poor but you were to be clean and live in a neat, orderly home. This resulted in a peaceful environment and a feeling of lightness that everyone entering our home felt.

We rarely went to a doctor. Toots knew about herbs and Castors' Oil. Of course there were the bi-yearly cleanses. One after Halloween and the other following Easter vacation. All the candy and junk we consumed during those holidays was flushed out of our systems. It was felt too much sugar from candy and sweets as well as salt from snacks, would weigh us down and lead to unhealthy life styles. Today, this process would be called detoxing the body.

Our household was one of laughter, working together, games, and friends to play with. Even though poorly furnished, it was filled with light. We always had a sheltered place to sleep and food on the table. All were welcomed and what we had was shared. Toots set the tone. Never get angry. If you did, she said you lost the argument. Share what you have with your family, friends and neighbors. God will provide what you need. And devotions were a daily ritual, grace offering thanks at meals and nightly prayer before bed.

When I look back, I realize that our home calibrated at an above average rate. There was always love, laughter and a positive way to look at everything including life. Toots set the tone with her unconditional love and surrender to what was. She raised all of us to see the good in everyone and in ourselves. No matter who you were, looked like, or financial circumstances, you were treated with kindness.

My Calibration Levels

My friend Harriet invited me to attend a bi-yearly Meditation Retreat several years ago. One of the benefits in participating was an informative inspirational presentation by Orest, the main speaker. He's an amazing enlightened gentleman with tremendous insight.

Another blessing was having my energetic levels calibrated by William, an extraordinary individual. He used the David Hawkins Scale of Human Consciousness mentioned at the beginning of this chapter. Its numbers range from one to a thousand with six hundred being the beginning of enlightenment and one thousand being Christ-like, Buddha-like, and Krishna-like. Attaining below the two hundred level mark includes behaviors displaying anger, racism, fear, hopelessness, shame, apathy, etc.

As a person develops in awareness, he/she rises up the scale. It's important to remember not to compare yourself to anyone else. You're striving to expand your own consciousness. We're here in an Earthly environment to nurture and develop in spirit through our experiences. We mature within by cultivating a non-judgmental attitude and becoming more loving of others. The more joy, peace and acceptance of things we cultivate, the higher our energetic body's calibration will register.

There were a few milestones for me. Unconditional love was the goal level I sought to achieve. It's amazing how I changed. No longer did material possessions seem important. I became content within understanding that I already had everything needed, not necessarily wanted. Taking the time to really look at others and what they were experiencing here in this lifetime helped me understand how truly blessed I was.

Planet Earth is a school all of us come to for an adventurous journey. If we're here to continually develop and expand, then we have to grow from the situations we encounter. Having an experience and learning from it allows us to move a step forward on our life path. If we don't learn from the event, we will repeat it until we do.

Understanding this concept was also a real eye opener. Even if we moved on from the experience the first time, the Universe will eventually repeat the lesson to make sure we 'did' master it. In reading the book _Oneness_ by _Rashi,_ I became aware of a pattern repeated over and over again. People involved would be different, the scenario slightly varied, but with the same outcome each time. Becoming aware of the pattern, meant I had a choice to make, I could continue the behavior or learn from it. Nothing ever goes away until it teaches us what we need to know. So, I chose to learn from it and ceased the repeated behavior.

BLOOD PRESSURE TEST

Another discovery concerned calibration level milestones. As we approach a new frequency level, the Universe or ego/mind will play games. It will test to see if we are ready for the next level.

The first test I remember involved my blood pressure. It usually ranged around one hundred-fifteen over seventy-two. As an Empath, I occasionally assume someone else's blood pressure issue. When that happens and there's extreme pressure in my head, I'll use the blood pressure gauge to see the numbers. If I'm experiencing pressure that belongs to someone else, the machine will usually register an error. It won't give me a reading. Just to make sure the pressure gauge is not malfunctioning, I'll ask my husband to take his pressure. It always gave him a reading. Then I'll go into meditation and calmness to reduce the pressure within myself and to help the person having issues. An ice pack on the nape of the neck is also helpful.

> One particular time when the intense pressure resulted in a massive headache, I called family and close friends asking how they were doing. No one was having problems but the heaviness continued. When I used the gauge to see if it would give me numbers, I was stunned. They were quite high registering one hundred eighty-nine over one hundred-ten. The fact that it gave me a reading was a good indication I might be the one having the problem.
>
> There was no logical reason for those numbers. An immediate reaction was to examine my food intake. Nothing had change. I was eating my usual diet with no additional high sodium items. Next I tried lowering the pressure by meditating for twenty minutes, going to peace within. But the headache still existed. Over the period of several days, nothing tried would lessen the pressure gauge numbers.
>
> As the intense pressure in my head came and went, I decided to keep a log of the readings. For the next ten days, at the same time each morning I wrote the numbers in a journal. When finally getting around to analyzing them, I had to laugh. Every third day, the recorded pressure was my normal self. The other days it was

extremely high. What if this was a test? The ego was having fun and games with me. As soon as I comprehended the mind's involvement, the pressure left. Interestingly, at no point was I concerned about the possibility of a stroke resulting from my abnormally high blood pressure readings. I was merely curious about what was occurring and why.

Just as individuals can have their energy calibrated, so can our country and our planet. War calibrates low and brings darkness. Peace and harmony bring light scoring higher. Remember, energy is neutral, it follows thought. What is within our consciousness can be manifested on the outside. Send out peace and blessings and peace and blessings come back to you. Send out criticism and discord and you will have a hostile environment creating fear which calibrates at a low level. Our free will allows us all to make choices as an individual and as a nation.

Chapter 6

LAY MINISTRY TITLE

God doesn't call the equipped...God equips the called.

Rick Yancey

I was raised in a religious household. Our family went to church every Sunday, sometimes twice if there was an afternoon or evening service too. Going to church felt as natural as waking up in the morning.

As youngsters, we attended a Sunday School that taught stories found in the Bible. Some of them were difficult to digest. Virgin conception was one. How did Mary get with child? She was not married and had never known a man yet she birthed a baby.

The Biblical reference acknowledging Jesus as fully human and fully Divine was another. How could he be both? Jesus was born of Mary, an Earthly Mother which meant he was human. His father was not an Earthling, but a heavenly Being, that indicated he was also Divine. Does this mean Jesus was of mixed parentage?

Another questionable occurrence is in the Book of Genesis. Two stories are written about Adam's creation. In one version he's formed from the dust of the ground. In the second he's created by the breath of God. This suggests a two body theory. Does one creation represent man's physical form and the other our spirit or consciousness? If so, as descendants of Adam we are also born with the same two bodies, a physical one and a spiritual one.

We're encouraged to faithfully accept all that's written in the Bible. As a teenager, I began to question Christianity. It was one thing to be taught stories that sometimes stretched the imagination, but the Bible was used to justify slavery in America. This was difficult for me to accept. I viewed God as one of love and peace. Religion was teaching that he was a vengeful god of war and enslavement.

Rev. Dr. Jeanne was organizing a two year Bible Study Certification class at her church. She called and asked if I'd be interested in attending. This seemed like a great opportunity to learn more about Scripture. Exposure to Biblical stories like Noah's Ark and Jonah and the Whale were part of Sunday School training as well as memorizing verses from the Book of Psalms. Weekly sermons included passages from both the Old and New Testament, but most ministers tended to have favorites. This was an occasion to read and interpret the entire content.

The course work was fascinating. Formal dissection of each book of the Bible became weekly assignments. Learning about the writers and historic facts from the time it was written placed a different slant on the teachings. This written work had survived thousands of years.

Old Testament writings basically portray the history of a vengeful God. In the New Testament, the birth of Jesus ushers in a God of love and peace. Although I originally signed on for one year, the classes were so interesting I agreed to do the second year as well.

Daniel's gift of prophesy and Joseph's dream interpretation ability were familiar stories. Scripture telling these gifts as well as others were endowed by the Holy Spirit put them in perspective. All of us knew people with exceptional talents such as artists, dancers, orators, etc. Discovery that a gift of healing was also biblically bestowed by the Holy Spirit became my 'Aha' moment.

Near the end of our two year class schedule, the Reverend in charge mentioned we were being ordained in two weeks. The purpose of studying the written word was to further qualify people interested in becoming integral members of their congregations as Elders, Evangelists and Ministers. In my particular case, it was simply to absorb the teach-ings, not get a title. I not only didn't want to become an ordained min-ister, I had no interest in becoming an elder or evangelizing. No way would this ceremony happen.

A little background info is necessary at this point. Before enrolling in the course, I refused to do healing sessions outside of my immediate family. In studying for my Reiki Master Teacher Certification, I became aware of certain state regulations. Qualifying as a medical professional, licensed therapist, or lay minister was required to perform laying on of hands. Not having any of these pieces of paper and being uncomfortable working on anyone outside family, this became a legitimate excuse to say no to requests.

Over the next week with continuous thought and a lot of soul searching, the humor of the situation hit me. I'd been using the excuse that I lacked a piece of paper certifying me as a therapist, medical professional, or minister to avoid helping people. Divine Source knew I wasn't going to train for the first two so it gave me a Lay Minister title.

The Universe has a great sense of humor. It handles what need to be done in its own way. In my case, it was smooth and painless. There were no hitches or snares. I simply surrendered and became a licensed Ordained Minister even though I never intended to use the title in a traditional role.

There's really not much choice when it comes to listening and obeying where the Creator is concerned. Universe has had a lot of fun with me in the past, but I am still in awe of incidents and events that occur. Who would've thought I'd be enrolled in an accredited two year Bible Study Certification program. You can't imagine my shock and bemusement at becoming a woman of the cloth. I bet heaven was smiling when it happened.

What I've found is one's destination is pre-determined. Our course is set. We arrive right on schedule. What is optional is the level of pain, disease and discomfort we choose to experience along the way.

There seems to be a substantial relationship between our thoughts, emotions and the state of our physical being. We choose what we wish to create and experience along the way. But, we must also discover answers to situations within ourself because knowledge comes from having lived the lesson. This is why I say all experiences are lessons. They help us become who we are.

Now that I'm qualified to perform laying on of hands, I've used my gift to present a series of Reiki sessions and Healing Hands workshops for relatives and friends. Participants learn to use the energy from their palms to facilitate healing on themselves as well as others. Amazing isn't it?

Chapter 7

RELIGION / SPIRITUALITY

What's the difference between religion and spirituality? That's a question I've thought about many times. I consider religion a tool used to unite people by giving them a common purpose or doctrine. Faith based communities also incorporate the social component humans need to avoid loneliness.

Once people are willing to adhere to the teachings of the theologians, rules are put into place. Followers are then encouraged to abide by these standards or commandments. Of course, in the process of setting up this organization, a hierarchy is established. Someone or a group of officials must see that regulations are followed for the good of all participants.

There must also be a leader. Usually it's a charismatic individual, or a person given command by the divine right of the strongest most persuasive leader in the area. This pious individual becomes a communicator between the people and their heavenly host. So, to get to God, you must have an intercessor or go between.

In Christianity, the Bible tells us that Jesus is the way to the Father. Of course, to get to Jesus you must go through the priest, minister, pastor, etc. Ranking order flows from God and Jesus at the top down to the clergy and last but not least, everyone else. Congregations must have places deigned worthy of worship such as cathedrals, synagogues, mosques, etc. These facilities must be maintained, hence–'Tithing'. Communicants must pay to support all facets of their faith based community.

Thus, religion becomes a way of life. "No one comes to the Father except by me", the Bible tells us Jesus said. Who is Jesus? The son of God, the God incarnate, the God in human form. Or, is he a Prophet or Master, One divinely connected to hearing the voice beyond the clouds.

What is spirituality? The realization that religion is not found in rites or ceremonies. It's a personal experience. Devout individuals believe you may speak directly with the Creator. An intercessor or go between is unnecessary. *Matthew 6:6 ...whenever you pray, go into your own room and close the door and pray to your Father who is in secret, and your Father who sees what is in secret will reward you...* Spiritualists believe you have a direct line. Prayer is talking to God, meditation is listening to Him. This two-way conversation can take place at anytime and anywhere.

What is the difference between religion and spirituality? Religion says you must have a liaison *(priest, pastor, minister, rabbi, etc)* who will intercede with God on your behalf. Spirituality says all people, believers and non-believers alike may communicate with the Divine directly. Religion is concerned with practices and beliefs. It give importance to words, rituals and material things. Spirituality doesn't need buildings or hierarchy of leadership and it doesn't cost money thus, tithing is not necessary.

Spirituality or Religion, it's lot to think about. If Pisces was the age of religion, then Aquarius might be the age of spirituality. This transformational shift from one zodiac sign to another has shown climate change altering the face of the Earth and an erosion in social structures around the globe. There's been an increase in terrorism, partisan politics, racism and general fear mongering. Going through this change will lead some people to look forward to and others to fear the change and want to maintain the status quo. Drug use and suicide, as well as depression and anxiety may also increase. As we move from one zodiac age to another it's bringing out the best and the worst of our world, but change is inevitable. It will come whether we welcome it or not.

Nature treats all the same so does the global pandemic caused by the Covid-19 Virus. Rain falls indiscriminately throughout the land. The sun shines on everyone. When an earthquake occurs or a tsunami comes, there is no differentiation between Christians and non-Christians; between the religious, the spiritualists and the non-believers. Man separates and religions differentiate, the Divine Source does not. We are all 'One' in God's sight.

Chapter 8

SOUND OPTIONS

My encounter with the sound of Oneness occurred one evening as I was relaxing in my den. 'OM' is a sacred chord in Hinduism and Buddhism as well as other Indian religions. Devotees use it in chanting and consider it the greatest of all mantras. I knew about the tone from readings and was really curious about it. In meditation classes and on recorded tapes, people incant it in affirmations and blessings. I've even tried to duplicate them. But, I've never been sure which utterance was the sacred version. Different presenters offered a variety of tonal variations. Sometimes it would be uttered in one syllable and at other times with two or three. There were also different first vowel stressing of 'OM'. In Sanskrit, it seems to be composed of three syllables 'A-U-M'.

SOUND OF ONENESS

The evening was so peaceful that after away putting the book I was reading, I reclined in a comfortable position. Noises of one sort or another were heard without conscious thought. After a while, I sensed my hearing alter. My right ear stayed the same with its usual resonance but my left ear developed a vacuum. All activity ceased, making my ear canal feel like an empty echo chamber. Of course, this instantly got my attention. I wondered what was happening now.

Something whispered in my left ear. It was so faint I had to really concentrate. Then I heard "OM". It was very soft at first, before becoming a bit louder. Remaining quite still, I listened intently trying not to disturb the incantation. Although I tried, it was impossible to duplicate the hum and listen at the same time so I stayed quiet.

It was really soft and melodious. The gentle mantra lasted for what seemed like a couple of minutes but was probably only a few seconds. As quickly as it came, "OM" left. Both ears returned to their usual tones.

Now I know what Oneness is supposed to sound like and that it's an angelic chime coming from above. I still can't reproduce it, but I'll know it if I ever hear it again. My editor Angela, wondered if OM has a frequency level. That perhaps when we rise to the level of that calibrated vibration, we can tune in and hear it. Oneness, a sacred melody that unites us to the voice of the Universe. Amazing!

SHUTTING OFF SOUND

A television program was broadcasting a couple of topics my husband thought I would be interested in watching. The first part was on voter machine tampering in an attempt to alter the 2012 presidential election results. The other segment concerned the Lynching History Museum in Montgomery, Alabama. It highlights the era from enslavement to mass incarceration of Black citizens in America. I'd already seen pictures and heard stories about the Museum. Since I couldn't watch it for more than a couple of minutes the first time it was televised, I certainly didn't want to see it again.

I cannot mentally handle brutality. My eyes are usually closed during violent scenes on television or in the movies. Sports activity that caused injury is difficult for me to tolerate. Of course it goes without saying that I don't watch real life war movies or horror ones. Witnessing pain being inflicted in any form is repugnant. This is especially true of slavery and its aftermath. During the Jim Crow period people were victimized by empowered citizens and law enforcement. Movie and television clips showed people with picnic baskets enjoying the entertainment of watching a person of color being hung from a tree until dead.

When the television in my den was turned on the 60 Minutes program video appeared, but with no sound. Both the regular channel and the hi-def channels had no audio. All of the others channels were fine. When I told my husband, he came up to try to get sound, but nothing happened. I now had a legitimate excuse not to watch the show because audio wasn't available. When my daughter was told about it, she laughed and said I had shut it off.

Question: Did I subconsciously shut off the audio portion? The answer is a resounding yes. In my choice of watching and hearing tales of pain and distress, 'No Sound' became an option I utilized. Of course the next day all channels were working fine.

Chapter 9

EYES CLOSED

My earliest recollection as a young child was having two deeply rooted fears, being burned to death and drowning. The first brought an alertness of anything that could cause a fire. The second required learning to swim well enough to survive should I fall into deep water. Not only did I take swimming classes, as a parent, my children were sent to camps that gave lessons. They and eventually my granddaughter became good swimmers. With age came the realization, those tragedies may have happened in previous lives.

As a youngster, I wasn't very talkative in order to avoid attracting unwanted attention. When I felt anxious because I foresaw things that might happen before they occurred, it was kept quiet. We were a church going family and it was best that no one knew my intuitive thoughts. This was interesting, because the Christian Bible *(1st Corinthians, Chapter 12)* tells us the Holy Spirit gave gifts of prophecy and healing to people. Several years ago in conversation with a friend, I mentioned my ability to assist someone's healing by placing my hands on the problem area. I thought she would be positively amazed at this. Instead she reacted as if I had a disease and couldn't get away from me fast enough. Her reaction only reinforced my belief to continue to stay silent.

Reaching adulthood it was instinctive to use herbs and hands on techniques with close family members while avoiding sessions with anyone else. But to be perfectly honest, I wasn't sure how these things worked. In my case it was try a remedy and hope for the best. Inherent gifts don't come with a primer telling you what to do.

It's not the situation that occurs that's important, but how we respond to it. There have been occasions when I was really afraid in attempting to accomplish something. Full of trepidation about what others would say. Frightened of not being successful would deter my even trying. Eventually came the understanding that my worrying was about the consequence of failure, humiliation and shame. With considerable thought, came the discovery of being distressed for no reason. I had to learn to face what I feared. What's the worst that could happen? If I succeed, great. If I fail, start again.

Learning not to dread, but just accept what happens from experiencing a lesson was greatly freeing. If life is an illusion, then altering the narrative can change one's perception of everything. Live and let live. Do what you can and leave the rest to the Universe. Let Go and Let God!

Home remedies ensured my children were healthy. Most of the time, I just listened to my gut feelings; however, advice was never offered to others. My greatest unease about helping anyone outside of our household was people assuming healing abilities beyond my capacity. This was an excuse to avoid working with outsiders. After reading _A Course in Miracles_, came the understand that healing is an inside job. People have to desire getting well and learn to go within to help themselves. There are many forms of restoring health. Most individuals want immediate physical healing, but the cure might be emotional, mental, and/or spiritual.

LETTER FROM BEYOND

Divine Source takes over when necessary. During pregnancy, the smell of meat in any form would result in severe nausea and almost losing consciousness. To survive, my sense of smell during carrying my children disappeared. It wasn't really lost, merely shut off mentally.

Refusal to see other's health issues by ignoring them led to me slowly going blind. This entire situation was fascinating. Being adamant about not seeing outsiders, was the beginning of having eye issues such as blurring, floaters, night vision, etc. Concern about this meant scheduling an eye examination with an Ophthalmologist. The doctor found no real issues.

A couple of months after the eye doctor visit, I received a letter addressed to my Mother. She had died almost 30 years prior. This was unusual. It was sent to my home. Toots lived in a different city from me. There would have been no forwarding mail listing. Receiving it was a real mystery.

Three of us were going to visit relatives in another state that weekend. When we arrived, I told family at the gathering about the letter. My sister laughed. She said since I refused to see or hear any attempts to use my healing abilities, the Universe sent a letter from beyond to get my attention. Quite obviously it did. This was a source of great hilarity throughout the entire weekend.

That Sunday evening, it was dark and raining when we left to return home. My husband said he couldn't drive. He had been diagnosed with night vision problems and needed cataract surgery. My niece who rode with us also couldn't drive. She experienced night blindness too. So this meant I became the designated driver. It was dark, raining and I also had eye concerns.

When we got into the car to drive home, I asked the Holy Angels to get us there safely. This was a one hundred plus mile drive to our destination. Fortunately, I was familiar with the highways, but my vision was blurred the entire way. Upon arriving safely home, I sincerely thanked the Angels for their assistance.

I took my luggage upstairs to put everything away before walking into the bathroom to rinse my face. My vision was still blurred. Suddenly, what could only be described as a force, slammed my head into the edge of the bathroom door. The side of my head hit at an angle culminating in instant sharp pain. Holding my head in both hands, I looked around to find the source. Instantly came the realization my vision had cleared. The blurring was gone. Raising my eyes up to heaven I murmured, "WOW now I can see!"

My immediate concern was that I'd have a pounding headache and probably a black eye none of which happened. From that knock on the head, my vision cleared up completely. No headache developed and my eye didn't turn black and blue. Although it was a blessing to have good vision again, I still thought, couldn't you have found another way to do this besides knocking my head up against a door.

The Divine Source has its own way of handling things. It also has a great sense of humor. Making me seem like I was going blind and sending that letter from beyond really got my attention. It made sense to me that if I could shut down my sense of smell to avoid becoming nauseous why not alter my sense of sight to avoid seeing other people's issues. That was a moment of wondering if there was a way we could have limited control over our five senses when necessary.

Part 2

Chapter 10

WHAT ARE ETHERIC CORDS?

*Cutting cords doesn't mean you want to
remove someone from your life. It's simply a means of
altering the relationship.*

Interacting with people, encourages the development of energetic connections known as 'Etheric Cords'. Energy moves along
these strings of attachment both toward one another and from one
another. People can have multiple cords affixed to them at the same
time. This means that others can attach our energy supply for their own
needs, leaving us feeling tired and drained. We can also do the same
thing to them.

Energy connections do exist. We can't see the electric wires but
information is sent and received using wireless mobile phones. People
can't see Etheric cords either, but we can feel their effect on our body. In
the Christian Bible (Gospel of St. Luke 8:45-46), Jesus knew instantly
when the woman touched the hem of his garment. Even though he
didn't see her, he felt an energy transfer.

> *Years ago when a relative was having medical problems and
> often hospitalized, she would tap into my energy. When this hap-
> pened, my body would become physically drained. I knew what
> was happening, but recognized her need for the extra boost to*

survive her health challenges. At the time, I was consciously open to allowing her access when she needed it. As her medical condition improved, I shut off her ability to tap into my energy at will.

If you've ever walked into a room full of people and suddenly felt exhausted, someone has tapped into your energy. This can happen anytime and anywhere. Sometimes your vocabulary will let you know when it takes place. You'll say or think you're mentally drained and need a break. Or you'll say or think you feel suddenly worn out and need to sit. You might even feel fatigued for no reason you can think of and want to take a nap.

Etheric cords can vary in thickness depending upon our relationships to the other individuals. There is the saying that people come into your life for a reason, a season, or a lifetime. When we're born into a family (*lifetime*), we're connected to our parents, siblings, and relatives with thicker cords than one attached to someone we once dated (*season*). We may also have a thinner connection with a colleague at work or our family physician (*reason*). They can appear in colors too. The Holy Bible (*Ecclesiastes, Chapter 12*) tells of a silver cord.

On some level we may have given permission for the person to attach to us. Often it can be us that hangs onto the other person. We can release these cords when they no longer serve our highest good. Cutting them in no way diminishes the relationship, but it can alter our emotional connection. Someone can still be in our life, but no longer have the same energetic emotional attachment.

Not only are there connections between us in our current life journey, they're also linked with other people across past lives. In other words, these cords are a major source for keeping our karmic lessons active and shared from lifetime to lifetime.

LETTING GO OF WHAT NO LONGER SERVES OUR HIGHEST GOOD

As we grow and develop, it can be time to let people go or for them to let us go. Remember, just as energy can pass from us to them, it can also transfer in reverse from them to us. It's a two-way street. How the current runs can often depend upon the situation and the relationship such as: parent to child, client to doctor, congregation member to minister, etc. Cord cutting is simply one way of helping us let go of relationships that no longer serve our highest good or to change the energetic dynamics of the relationship.

Cutting one doesn't indicate abandoning or disowning, it's merely a method of releasing and altering the relationship. Moving on means letting people go energetically. The result will affect both parties. We don't lose any memories or thoughts, just changing and releasing a power connection we no longer need.

Cords can be severed with any person who causes us anxiety or stress. If we find the person always intrudes on our thoughts and emotions, it might be better to alter the relationship by removing the cord attachment. This will help clear our energy field or aura.

Abusive people who physically and emotionally affected our lives can also be cut away. If those cords remain in place they can cause depression, withdrawal and quite possibly even illness. Once the cords are removed, psychological and spiritual links will begin to lessen and eventually any anxiety or stress we might have experienced will begin to dissipate.

It's important to recognize when another person may be disrupting one's energy. Sometimes there's a feeling of carrying a great weight on our shoulders. This may be an indication that there are lines attached to us that need to be cut.

Jennifer O'Neill in her book _Pursuit of Happiness,_ said that letting go is one of the hardest things for people to do, yet it is one of the most beneficial things they will ever do for themselves.

CAREGIVER CORD CUTTING

When you become the major care giver for a family member or friend, a weight begins to settle on your shoulders. The more responsibility for the person and the longer you're accountable, the heavier the feeling becomes.

> _Looking out for my Mother (Toots) was my conscious decision. She needed support financially and emotionally. Her worries became my worries. Whenever she called, I answered. Whatever she needed, I tried to supply. My reasons were really quite simple. She birthed me. I existed here on Earth because of her and my deceased Father. During my youth, she was always there for me. Because she wanted to maintain her independence, I had to create a second job_

in order to support her. Of course, I had Divine Angelic assistance,
I could never have done it by myself.

   High blood pressure was a major health concern. At first I tried
to alter her diet, but she was a bacon and eggs or sausage and eggs
breakfast person. She ate all kinds of meat and fried foods for lunch
and dinner. My concern for her health was making me become a
nag until one day it dawned on me. Toots was now in her late six-
ties and always had a smile on her face. I tried to get her to move in
with me but she wouldn't. She enjoyed her home, her neighbors, her
friends, and her church. So I stopped nagging. I let it go. She lived
to be seventy-four years old and died instantly from a major stroke.
When she transitioned, I felt lighter. It was as if a weight had been
removed from my body.

When you've done all you can to help and be supportive to someone,
when they transition, you automatically feel the cord sever. The link
between you and that person no longer exists in this lifetime. That's
the relief of etheric weight loss or removal felt. I experienced lightness
because her etheric cord attachment no longer existed.

A MOTHER'S GRIEF

I accompanied Lois on a visit to her grief counselor approximately
a year following the death of her middle son, Lamont. She had been
having problems accepting the loss and asked me to go with her.

   In listening to her conversation with the counselor, I realized
Lois was suffering not only from the death of this son. She had
never completely mourned the death of her youngest son, many
years prior. When Billy was ill, she felt she had no choice but to
continue working for the health benefits. It was agony watching
her youngest son's health slowly deteriorate and not be able to help
him. Lamont, the son who just transitioned had been his brother's
primary caregiver.

   This time Lois decided to retire from work to be with her son
during the final stage of a four year battle with cancer. She now qual-
ified for both pension and social security benefits. After Lamont's
passing, she blamed her job for not allowing her to take a year off
to be with him in the beginning stages of his illness.

On the way back from the grief counselor visit, Lois talked and I listened. She was feeling bitter toward her former employer, blaming the job. I mentioned it was her choice to stop working the employer didn't fire her. It was important for her to see it wasn't the job. She was mourning the transition of this son as well as the passing of her younger one too. As we talked, she acknowledged that fact. During the time Billy was ill, she couldn't handle losing him. He was only in his twenties. It was a difficult time for her as a parent. Going to work everyday helped maintain her sanity.

Lois continued to talk about her former employer as well as other things that bothered her. She was still feeling bitter about how unfair life was. I asked her if she would like an energy session before going home. She agreed. It was a twenty-five minute technique basically interacting with her emotional state of mind. As my hands rested on her, I could sense her body becoming calm. At the conclusion, she said it felt as if other hands were touching her too. Now she was in a very peaceful state.

During the trip home, Lois experienced a cord cutting. While driving through the park, an etheric cord severed and left her body. She suddenly saw a large shimmering silver string float out of her car windshield up toward the sky. As she watched, she said her body felt fifty pounds lighter. Anger toward the job dissolved leaving feelings of being cleansed and at peace. She drove home as if floating on air. Mentally and emotionally she had cut an Etheric Cord, letting go of a weight that laid heavy on her heart. She couldn't recall much more about the drive. The next thing she remembered was parking the car in front of her house. Lois was now at peace.

EMOTIONAL ATTACHMENT

A friend Holly, needed to sever a cord attaching her to a close relative. Their relationship had become a drain on her energy. In conversation with her, I suggested that she do an Etheric Cord cutting. It would alter the relationship between herself and the other individual. She voiced concern about the effect of their relationship on her health both physically and emotionally.

Holly decided to perform the etheric cord cutting. She lit the candle and followed the procedure, (Appendix A) with the exception that I asked her to write the person's name on a piece of paper. At the end of the ceremony she was to burn the paper similar to the Forgiveness Exercise (Appendix B).

After doing the cord cutting, Holly tried to burn the paper. It wouldn't burn. The atmosphere became so smoky, it set off her kitchen's smoke alarm. When she called to tell me, I suggested she redo the exercise. The paper had to burn completely for the relationship to alter. She did the procedure several more times. Each time the paper would burn slowly leaving a bit unburnt. The final time she did it, the paper quickly burned a bright white yellow and blue flame. When the fire extinguished the paper was completely incinerated.

Holly felt an immediate change in their relationship. She felt lighter and the other person also felt the difference. Their relationship became less tension filled and more peaceful. Nothing happens in isolation. Cord cutting like forgiveness affects both parties.

Cord Cutting

There are different ways to cut cords. Use the following suggested methods or change to what feels right and comfortable to you. What is important is your Intention.

Find a quiet peaceful private place to do this. Light a candle, say a prayer and go into a meditative or prayerful mode. Do not rush. It's important to feel relaxed.

State your Intention to cut the Etheric Cord attachment with whomever you name. Then proceed to have a one-sided conversation with the individual. Speaking from the heart, say everything necessary to affect closure with that relationship. When your talk is concluded, let him/her know that it is time to let them go.

Now imagine yourself cutting the connections. Remove them from your back, front and everywhere around your body. Perform a scissor motion using your fingers and wrist. Even though you can't see the cords they do exist.

When you finish say a prayer, blow out the candle and remain in the meditative or prayerful mode for a bit longer. Mentally again thank the person whose etheric cord you cut for being in your life. Let him/her know that you are grateful for having known him/her and wish them well.

Chapter 11

Forgiveness ~ and ~ Attachments

Giving true forgiveness is receiving peace within yourself.
When you forgive from the heart, you feel light within.

A Course in Miracles

Another way to detach Etheric Cords is through a Forgiveness Exercise. The act of forgiving helps to free the soul. The past is just that, over and done with. It's past history. Learn the lessons, accept the situations and move on. Our past experiences can never come back to haunt us unless we keep them alive in current times by recalling the event to memory.

Forgive those who we feel have caused us any pain, injury or anxiety. Most of the time they didn't realize the extent of what they did. They've usually forgotten about it while we're still remembering the pain it caused. We forgive a person's action to remove it from our minds, not theirs. The Four Agreements by Don Miguel Ruiz tells us to never take things personally. Keeping an unpleasant encounter alive within us can cause stress. Stress leads to dis-ease. It can eat away at flesh like a cancer. The individual who caused concern might just have been having a bad day. Making you feel upset could have been unintentional on his/her part. If you internalize it, you nourish a situation that the other person might have already let go.

Forgiveness goes in two directions. Sometimes it's for us to pardon others for something we feel they've done to cause us distress or pain and at other times we may have to ask for understanding. Have you ever said or done something in the heat of the moment and later regretted? It's important to offer ourselves the same mercy we offer others. In the 'Our Father' prayer we say: *Forgive us our trespasses as we forgive those who trespass against us.*

When someone comes into our life in a significant way, they are attached to us by an Etheric Cord. These are invisible attachments. Some are thin while others are various degrees of thickness depending upon the relationship involved. It's important to know when it's time for a family member, a friendship or an acquaintance to be let go. We need to remove their attachment. These cords can be cut forever or just be exchanged to another type of connection. Some cords are shared because of karmic actions carried over from a former lifetime. It's important to let those individuals go. Letting go in this lifetime means you'll be free of their entanglement in your next re-birthing experience.

RECURRING DREAM

Betty had a recurring dream for years about being assaulted during World War II. She was born after the war had ended and couldn't imagine why she felt that fear of attack. In a conversation with me, whom she had just met for the first time, she brought up the subject. It was important to her as well as a mystery since she hadn't had any abusive experiences in her current life.

I suggested she do the Forgiveness ritual as a means of letting it go and halting the recurring dream. After we talked, I sent her the format. A couple of weeks later she performed the exercise. She said it was amazing how light her body felt afterwards. Doing the Forgiveness ritual released the trauma associated with the incident that had affected her daily life. I haven't asked her, but the dream should also have left when she completed absolved the people or person involved. The exercise severed a cord attached from a past lifetime.

Forgiveness is an amazing thing. With it we can transform darkness into light. We can release a cord altogether or we can simply change the dynamics of the relationship. As we become attuned to our life's priorities, we can selectively weed out people and activities. It's important to let go of people who try to coerce us to accommodate their personal preferences. They only serve to drain our energies and distract our focus.

By being open and honest about our own progress, we can help others with whom we share the journey. During our time here on Planet Earth, we'll face many storms and trials, but if we learn to forgive, we become a shining example for others to see.

Author Nicki Scully in his book <u>Alchemical Healing</u> says, forgiveness is releasing rather than accepting. It frees up energy that's been holding stressful patterns in place. Removing them through amnesty allows us to clear ourselves of unwanted attachments and to have more energy.

DESTINY, FATE, KARMA

Our destination is pre-determined. Our course is set. We will be born right on schedule. What is open is what we choose to create and to experience along the way. We choose our response to the kind of life we'll have. Remember the Universe is like a mirror, what you send out is what's returned to you.

Destiny is what will ultimately occur. Time and place of our transition or death will happen when we're destined to do so. Fate is how we live until the destined transition occurs. It's our free will choices or forks in the road. Turning right will lead to one path and turning left will lead to another. Karma is the spirit within us that we share with the outer world. It's the Golden Rule. Do unto others as you would have them do unto you. What goes around comes around.

Throughout our life, we'll make choices. Some we can enjoy and others we might regret. But in the end, I believe destined events will most certainly occur. We come to Planet Earth to learn through experiences and to grow in consciousness.

Surrendering to forgiveness is the key to moving on in life. It's a means of letting go of the past. You have to mean it with all of your heart, mind and soul. The Divine Source knows if you are sincere.

DATING ABUSE

Occasionally at an outside event I would come in contact with a young lady. Stella was a lovely gentle individual. Whenever we met, she would have a smile on her face. In getting to know her I realized she offered a friendly look to everyone, but after a brief moment sadness would replace it.

An opportunity to sit and talk with her happened one day. The first question out of my mouth was, "Why are you so sad"? She gave me a puzzled look and asked what I meant. I told her that even though she smiled there was a look of sadness in her eyes. By now we had built up a measure of trust so she felt comfortable speaking about what was bothering her.

Being a single young woman, she signed onto a dating site. Long story short, she went on a date with someone who sexually abused her. Unfortunately, this individual periodically visited in her neighborhood. He let her know he was looking forward to another date. She wasn't sure how to handle the situation.

I suggested she do the Forgiveness Exercise not for him, but for herself. Once she had the format, it became her decision. Apparently she mulled over the suggestion for a bit. Several weeks later I could tell she had done it. The next time we met, she gave me the biggest hug. The smile on her face included her eyes. Her inner peacefulness was obvious. When she burned the paper at the conclusion of the exercise, Forgiveness was complete. She felt the difference immediately. Stella was radiant. The dynamics of the relationship between her and the abuser changed. She could now move on.

REALISTIC DREAM

Remember, time and space can be relative. Using this application is also a way of communicating with someone who's deceased. There have been times when a loved one died before we had an opportunity to say goodbye. This is a perfect way to talk with that person and at the same time achieve peace within oneself. If you've been the victim of an injustice or abuse, here's another means for healing yourself. You can forgive the abuser or ask for forgiveness if you were the culprit.

Laura, had a dream about a close personal friend who was now deceased. She knew it was him even though she never looked directly into his face. He told her he came to take her back with him. In her dream they were walking through an area that looked like a wasteland. It was barren, scorched earth and lifeless.

They arrived at a building where they were met by a very large figure dressed in white. Her friend tried to take her in with him. The figure dressed in white said she couldn't enter, that she had to go back. Laura told her friend that if he needed her she would stay. But again, the guardian in white told her to go back. She woke up and couldn't go back to sleep.

In the morning she called to tell me about her dream and asked how to interpret it. Even though her friend died several years ago, he was still existing in that wasteland area. I said he probably felt unhappy about their relationship and his treatment of her. She would have to do the Forgiveness Exercise to help send him to the Light.

We made arrangements for her to do the procedure a couple of days later. I visited bringing all required items with me. Elements were arranged on her cocktail table. Before beginning she sat quietly on the sofa. It was necessary for her to go within and relax. When she felt ready she could proceed. This was between her and her deceased friend. All speaking had to be from her heart in order to put his spirit at rest. Giving her privacy, I went into another room to meditate.

About a half hour later, she was done. The emotional toll was quite visible. Her eyes were full of unshed tears. Concluding the Forgiveness is accomplished by disposing of the elements onto the soil for purification. I then smudged her living room area and both of us. Together we thanked the Divine Source and asked that a Light fill the vacuum created when her friend departed. Laura said she felt as if a great weight lifted off her body leaving her lighter and at peace.

Two nights later, she had another dream. Her friend came to visit again to say goodbye for now. He was dressed in a tan suit and his entire smiling face was visible. He presented her with a big bag of ripe yellow bananas.

Once again they were strolling through the same wasteland as before. However as they walked, the scenery began to change. A rising sun appeared making it a beautiful warm clear day. Yellow flowers began to bloom and grass started growing. Trees were visible as well as a body of calm blue water in the distance.

As they got near the building, her friend said it was time for him to leave. Laura said she would go with him. This time he was the one who told her she had to go back. In parting he let her know that he would see her again. She woke up, thought about the dream, and then went back to a sound peaceful sleep.

Her experience displayed how the Forgiveness affected both the giver and the recipient of the exercise. It was a way of healing both people involved. In the vast Universe, time and space are relative.

ASKING FOR FORGIVENESS

My Father passed away during my teen years. I was very upset and blamed him for leaving and God for taking him. He had cancer and during a short period of time lost a lot of weight. Basically, he faded away. The last time I saw him alive was at the hospital. He looked emaciated. Seeing him decline from a healthy six foot two individual to skin and bones was difficult to accept. I couldn't handle it and never went back for another visit.

Several decades later I had lunch with two of my sisters. While eating they began reminiscing about all of the activities Daddy had done with us. They were laughing, joking and talking about past events. According to them, I was present too. Even though I tried it was impossible to visualize those times and places. Memories were buried real deep inside. Suddenly it hit me. I'd emotionally blocked out most of my childhood.

The more I thought about the situation, the greater I felt the need to mend my relationship with him. Searching within, visions of a wonderful caring Father emerged. When I began to recall memories that were buried deep below the surface, I remembered him giving us allowances, buying us ice cream, laughing with my older sisters about some of their experiences, etc. How could I have forgotten him?

The Forgiveness Exercise seemed like a method I could use to thank him for everything. I decided to do a grave side visit. On a blanket placed down by his Memorial Head Stone I placed his picture, a wooden cross, fresh cut flowers, and a small bottle of champagne. Kneeling, I said prayers and asked for his forgiveness. I thanked him all that he had done during my short time with him. Please I pleaded, forgive me for taking so long to apologize. While there, I talked about things that had since happened bringing him up to date.

Ending my visit with the Our Father Prayer, I poured him a glass of champagne and sprinkled it over the grave. I thanked Daddy, his angels, his guides and all in his heavenly abode. His dying had been so painful that I'd completely erased almost all memories of my childhood because of it. I can't explain the lightness and sense of peace within at the completion of the Forgiveness Exercise. It had given me closure that I wasn't even aware I needed.

SUMMARY

There are many things in our lives that we hide in our subconscious mind. We push them way down into our memory bank. But everything that ever happened to us stays with us throughout our life time.

Two major things can alter our existence here on Planet Earth. First is unconditional love. I'm not talking about romantic love. Unconditional love means loving our brothers and sisters because they are creations of God. We might not always like their behavior but unconditional love does not judge.

The second is forgiveness. Forgiveness cleanses our soul. No matter how big the incident or how small, it works two ways. It frees both people, the individual who inflicted the hurt as well as the person who felt the pain.

Both of these traits are usually embodied by non-judgmental individuals. When you forgive from the heart, you send light, peace and unconditional love out into the world. And remember, what you send out is what will come back to you.

Chapter 12

KARMA

When someone comes at us, that's his karma.
How we respond becomes our karma.

Wayne Dyer

What is Karma and how does it work? Books I've read, describe it as a *Universal Law of Cause and Effect*. It's a system where what you do reflects back on you. The Bible tells us you reap what you sow. That means our fate is the result of both good and bad, based on one's actions as we go through life. If you are kind ~ kindness comes back. If you are angry ~ anger comes back.

I suggest to family members that they always send blessings to everyone and every incident. A car cuts you off, bless the driver and wish him safe travel. People at work get on your last nerve, bless them. One of the principles in Don Miguel Ruiz's book <u>The Four Agreements</u> is to not take things personally. You don't know what issues people are dealing with that may cause them to act unkind at work, school, or in public. Just 'bless them'.

WORK ENVIRONMENT

Delores called for advice about a work situation. She was becoming upset with a colleague's negative behavior. It was causing her to hate going to work and having to interact with this particular individual. After listening for a while, I asked if she would try something. Every time she saw the fellow worker to silently bless her. And I suggested blessing her office and work space on a daily basis. Send out only positive vibes towards the person. At first, she didn't want to do this. The last thing she thought about was being nice to someone who was constantly berating her. Remember, our karma is earned by our actions as we go through life. I asked her to try it for a week and then call me back.

A couple of weeks later she telephoned. Her voice sounded calm and relaxed. She'd done what I recommended. By blessing everyone and everything, her work atmosphere altered. The colleague was no longer abrasive. In fact, her co-worker mentioned some emotional issues she was dealing with outside of work. Blessings Delores sent out were coming back in the form of a more productive work environment.

We are born to experience life through various encounters bringing us lessons. Karma is created by how we respond. Retaliate hatefully or with anger and the consequences will be a return of hate and anger. Offering love and kindness will in turn shower us with love and kindness. We can choose to bless everyone and everything constantly. An old proverb says be kind to people you meet as you climb the ladder of success. They'll be the same ones you pass on your way down.

All life on Earth operates in a pattern or cycle. Vegetation like trees and flowers grow from seeds, survive for a period of time and then die only to repeat the cycle next growing season. Weather patterns also have repeating habits such as hundred year floods and storms.

People, animals, reptiles, insects, and plants also have cycles. We're born, live and die. Then we begin the process again. For some, life may be only a short interval of time. Others may survive a hundred years or more. Everything repeats a birth, life, death, and rebirth cycle.

All of our previous existences help make us what we are today. Each time we're reborn here on Planet Earth, fortune is accumulated by our words and actions. We also have a karmic bank from past life chances. Some karmic issues might be removed during our current life time. Others may remain in storage to become part of a future rebirthing.

If you were rich in a past life, you might be born into a poor family in your next life. If you had relationship issues in a past life, this might present an opportunity to work through them for a successful conclusion so you can move on. This is all speculation, but it could happen. All of our actions generate responses which will accumulate in karma.

For the past several years, sages and psychics began to feel the United States of America was going to experience something. They weren't sure exactly what or how. But, the feeling was that America would begin to experience predestined activity.

Karma refers to actions that lead to future consequences. The United States of America through its past actions of slavery, demonizing people based on race, gender and religion as well as greed is in the process of bearing the fruit of our past unjust behavior. Dr. Martin Luther King, Jr. said, "Darkness cannot defeat darkness only Light can do that." We are seeing darkness rise from the earth in the form of racism, hatred and anger. For our country to raise its consciousness level we must do as Dr. King said. Hate cannot defeat hate, only love can defeat hate.

We must as a nation forgive and ask for forgiveness. Be kind to all. Stay positive and refrain from any negativity in thought, word or deed. If we as a people raise our consciousness level, so will our country and ultimately our world.

Chapter 13

REINCARNATION

Recognition of the eternal nature of life...
Birth is not the beginning and death is not the end.

Circle of Miracles

There are people who have experienced heart failure and in some cases, been pronounced dead only to have re-awakened after various periods of time with their hearts beating again. They've had what is termed a Near Death Experience (NDE). Some of them have written books documenting what they observed during the NDE. This is not reincarnation, but it offers a glimpse of the Great Beyond. It offers an awareness there's a lot we don't know or understand. It also explores the possibility of there being life after death.

Birth ~ Death ~ Rebirth. This is the cycle of our earthly experience. Reincarnation is the belief we live, die and return to Earth in another body. It's the belief that there's no such thing as death, just an unending pattern where we live many lives as we progress along our spiritual path. We are born, we live, and then we transition from our current physical form. According to <u>The Power of Karma</u>, a book by Mary T. Browne, karma and reincarnation are completely interwoven. During each lifetime, we create karma through our thoughts and actions. When we reincarnate, we are given an opportunity to balance the karmic bank account accumulated during each of these rebirth cycles.

When a person is alive, the Divine spark called the soul is active. Even on the death bed, you still see the spark giving life and energy to the person. But when the person dies or transitions from the physical form, you see only a body or the costume the person wore. There is no spark, only a shape that resembles a lifeless mannequin. The energetic spark is gone and only a framework remains.

My belief is that all of us have a predestination here on planet Earth. It's a journey of experiencing many situations of joy, trauma, and lessons designed to help us develop mentally, emotionally and spiritually. All of our life involvements are for our growth and development. Accepting an encounter and learning from it allows us to proceed to the next lesson along our path. I believe there are no good or bad experiences, just actions for us to digest and learn from. It's never what occurs, but our reaction that's important. When knowledge is gained from the assignment we move on. However, if we don't master it we will repeat it.

Think about your own life or that of a close friend or relative. How many times have you had almost the exact same situation happen only with different cast members. Some things you only need to experience one time to say never again. Others, especially those involving our emotions, may occur several times before we learn our lesson.

When I think about our current Earthly sojourn I wonder: Did people come into this lifetime to experience being murdered, jailed, abused, addicted to alcohol, sex or drugs? Did children around the globe come to be enslaved workers at young ages? Youth who feel they aren't good enough because of parental demands and peer pressure come to commit suicide? Did entire families reincarnate to experience becoming refugees caused by wars where their possessions are stolen or destroyed? Are all of these situations part of our reincarnation's karmic payback? Were these judgments meant to erase pass karma debt in order to benefit our growth in consciousness?

Ultimately we're sent to Planet Earth to have challenges that will help us absorb the lessons of light and love before we can ascend from this birth, death, rebirth cycle. When rebirth occurs, our path and destiny will also include those special skills learned in prior reincarnations. People such as artists, musicians, healers, orators, etc. are born with talents they honed in previous lives.

Personal participations in all of our various reincarnations have made us who we are today. The key is to learn to accept the experiences we were sent here to learn in this lifetime's journey. Easy to say but difficult to sometimes comprehend. We must continue to grow and develop into spiritual beings filled with light and unconditional love for all humanity.

Chapter 14

TRANSITION OR DEATH

*Death is as unique as the individual who is
experiencing it. It comes in its own time; in its own way.*

Barbara Karnes

At one time or another during the aging process most of us think
about maintaining good health and dying. As a Hospice volun-
teer, I saw the precursor to both up close and personal. I discovered
there's a pattern to everything, even death. Based on eating and drinking
habits, you could observe the body start to shut down. Clients began to
lose their appetites and desire for food. They would proceed to slowly
consume less fluids. This loss of appetite and lack of thirst was often
accompanied by an unseen guest. Clients would have conversations
with visitors only they could see. I observed that someone usually
always came to help the individual transition from this Earthly home.
The hospice resident would stare at a spot in the room and talk with
someone they saw but was invisible to me. It was often a deceased relative, a deceased friend or a heavenly vision. But someone usually came
to help them make a peaceful transition.

One of the things that almost always happened when I visited
before the client departed, was being thanked for all of the things they
felt I had done. When visiting with clients, I usually took flowers or
magazines. Occasionally for cancer clients, I would take a selection of

scarves for them to wear. If asked, I would read to them from short story books or their favorite passage from the Bible. Generally, they just wanted a good listener. Clients could relieve their souls of things that had festered within for many years. It was easier to confide in a non-family member who wouldn't judge what was said. In the process of cleansing themselves, they could go to peace within.

POWER OF WORDS

We never know the power our words can have. One client in her late seventies, hadn't forgiven a sister who at the age of fourteen had uttered words that still resonated with her. They were having an argument and the sister said things in the heat of the moment that were never forgotten. After several visits with her, the client felt she could tell me about the unforgiving feelings she still held. Her sister was coming to visit later that day. She was ambivalent about seeing her.

My client talked and I listened. When she finished, I asked her if she wanted to take unkind feelings about anyone with her to heaven's gates. During our continuing conversation, she had an opportunity to look back and recall the teenage encounter. The client said she had no idea that this was the reason she always disliked her sister. As we talked and put things in perspective, she laughed and said it felt like a weight had been lifted. Feeling at peace now she looked forward to enjoying her sister's visit that afternoon.

HEALING HANDS

In another case, a hospice resident had an issue with the fingers of one hand. At my weekly visit she showed me that she could no longer bend one of her fingers. It happened suddenly she said a couple of days before. It was her right hand and she was having problems holding a fork to eat with. I asked if I could hold her hand. She said yes. Placing her hand in both of mine I began to gently massage her palm and fingers. I thought she might have jarred one of the bones out of joint. As I worked on her fingers she talked about her church. Members had visited earlier that day. She told me how

53

*much she appreciated the time and attention church members gave
her. By the time I departed, she was relaxed and falling asleep.*

*At my next visit, she held up her hand and wiggled her fingers.
She wanted to thank me for all I had done and especially healing
her finger. It's hard to explain, but from the way she talked, I knew
this was a goodbye. Later that day after another visit by her minister and members of her church death occurred.*

When I volunteered at hospice, I didn't try to heal anyone. My belief is
you die when it's your time. During my visits I silently prayed for clients
to have light, peace and unconditional love. In the case of that client, I
wanted to help her finger heal. I didn't think it was necessary for her to
be unable to use her hand until time to pass away.

I did experience a couple of my client's departures. In one instance,
a puff of smoke came out of the top of her head. In another instance, the
night one of my clients transitioned she came to visit in a dream. She
was a tiny figure dressed in pale blue with wings. But, clients seemed to
know when they were leaving and always said thank you and goodbye.

DEBRA'S GRIEF

*Her husband died after a short illness the year before. Debra
had withdrawn from almost everything. Friends encouraged her
to attend a session where I was presenting a workshop. I noticed
her sitting in the back of the room as I talked. Her eyes and smile
seemed to be so sad.*

*She called the next day to say how much she enjoyed my pre-
sentation. In talking with her, I asked why she was so sad. I mentioned that even though she smilies, it wasn't coming from within.
We talked for a bit and she told me about her husband's demise.*

*Thinking how to help reminded me that it was important for
her to let grief out. Not to keep thoughts and feelings locked inside.
I went to my neighborhood book store to find a journal. The book
cover should reflect her beautiful interior and also offer a bit of hope
for the future. When I found what I thought was the perfect journal,
I telephoned to say I was going to stop past and drop off something
for her. The next day I gifted her with the 'Remembrance' journal.
She was quite appreciative and teary and invited me in for a cup of*

tea. While we drank a pot of tea, I listened as she talked about her loss. This was the beginning of her healing process.

Here's the context of the note I placed in her journal:

I told her that her husband's spirit was always with her. Imagine how sad he must be when he sees how difficult it is for her to accept God's plan for him. Between birth and death everyone is on his/her life's path. You were blessed to have shared many years with him. God called your husband home, but your personal journey continues.

Please make use of this journal I selected for you. Write in it every time a thought comes of the life you and he shared. In recording your thoughts and feeling, hopefully you will find closure and acceptance of God's plan. And, only in your finding peace can your husband's spirit smile.

A week later, I received her thank you card with this message:

Thank you for my gift and your beautiful and inspiring note. I know that God has a plan for us all and I must accept that his plan for my husband was best for him.

I have begun to write in my journal today and gratefully appreciate your efforts to help me to overcome this sad feeling. Thank you for your love and grace.

A year later she sent this note:

I'm still writing in my remembrance book. It's becoming easier now and I am doing things that I enjoy. I sang with the Choir when they did the Messiah. It was a nice experience. But, I will always miss my husband deeply at Christmas.

ACCEPTING AND LETTING GO

Letting go. It's easy to say but not easy to do. When it's time to depart from this lifetime, the spiritual entity is looking forward to returning to the heavenly realm to rest, recover and prepare for its next reincarnation. Sometimes before they can depart this Earthly existence, they want or need their loved one's permission.

If a person emotionally close to them is not ready to accept their leaving, some patients linger until relatives can come to grips with their death. They want to make sure their loved ones are prepared to let them go. Sometimes the family is so grief stricken the soul lingers pass the time it thought it would need.

When a spiritual entity or soul is in physical form, it experiences all of the emotions humans are capable of. It feels joy, happiness, love as well as peace and harmony. But it can also feel anger, grief and pain. If suffering from a serious illness, the pain can be excruciating.

While volunteering at a hospice, occasionally I spoke with family members. If the patient was in extreme pain and ready to depart, I would let them know that their loved one was waiting for them to say the family would be fine and he/she could go in peace.

One situation involved an elderly woman. Her relatives came faithfully to be with her. Her son who was a physician was having a hard time dealing with her dying. He felt devastated that as a doctor he couldn't heal his Mother. In speaking with him, I suggested he look at the situation as one in which he was blessed to have had her for forty plus years. She was in pain and ready to leave but needed to hear he would be okay. The next day, he visited her and he told her he loved her and would see her again some day. She could depart in peace.

Death is interesting. It's the uninvited visitor most of the time. But, it will come regardless of your expectations. It has been described as a feeling of freedom where you move through a tunnel *(or take a boat)* and are met with unconditional love. We have to live our lives to the best of our abilities, and if we are wise, we graciously accept the spectrum of death when it comes. We don't know when or where or how, but it is inevitable.

Chapter 15

MEDITATION

Through the study of books, one seeks God.
By meditation one finds Him.

Padre Pio

Meditation is the art or technique for quieting the mind from endless thoughts and chatter. Our brains work twenty-four hours a day, seven days a week non-stop. There's a constant barrage of intrusive thoughts disturbing our conscious awareness. Introspection helps us quiet our mind. It requires practice and patience. But, the more we meditate, the easier it becomes.

We can define it as a practice in which our thinking is led toward inducing a state of awareness. It's an inward personal practice we must undertake ourselves that'll help make us more sensitive to what's truly important. In the silent mind, we try to become an observer in order to attain a level of detachment.

It's said that when we pray, we are talking to God. When we meditate, we're listening to His response. With consistent practice comes an awareness of a higher state of consciousness.

Religious and spiritual groups have practiced various forms of contemplative quietness since antiquity. It can be found across many cultures and traditions. The following scriptures are located in the King James Version of the Holy Bible: *"...for thou shalt meditate therein day and night" (Joshua 1:18); "Let the words of my mouth and the meditation of my heart be acceptable in Thy sight..." (Psalm 19:14)*

BRAIN WAVE LEVELS:

When you determinately enter into silent reflection, your brain waves shift. They fluctuate into deeper levels of consciousness. Varying frequencies allowing for differing degrees of concentration are:

> **Alpha**–Light sleep: meditation, intuition, no time and space limitation
>
> **Beta**–Awaken state: perception of time and space, increases logical thinking
>
> **Delta**–Deeper sleep and unconsciousness: facilitates healing
>
> **Gamma**–Intense focus: decreases anxiety and fear, increases positive emotions
>
> **Theta**–Associated with the 3rd eye: encourages creativity and problem solving skills

Alpha level is usually associated with meditation. The challenge for most people is staying there. Mental chatter and stray thoughts can easily disrupt a person's concentration. So can physical restlessness, pent up stress, and mental fatigue. Staying clearly focused is the key for putting your worries aside. As your stress melts away, your attentiveness can soar.

PURPOSE OF MEDITATION

It's said the purpose of this practice is to go within and create a quiet state of inner peace; to realize the spiritual presence within each of us. My meditation instruction sessions began when I enrolled in a night school class. One hour a week for seven weeks, the instructor encouraged us to relax our bodies and minds while breathing deep from the abdominal area. Each class was informative and included a different guided meditation. Her suggestion that we practice at home beginning with a ten-minute timed session was a good one. Any questions encountered during practice would be discussed at our next meeting.

When I began to meditate on a regular basis I discovered there were several stages of development. In the beginning, it was constant chatter. Things and events from the past that were thought long forgotten would suddenly pop into my head. And of course, this disrupted the quiet state of mind I was striving to achieve. The instructor said when this happened to accept the memory and let it go. Imagine putting the thought into a balloon and seeing it float up and away into the heavens.

Becoming present meant emptying the mind. With chatter, our thoughts were either of the past or the future yet to come. Just as I was able to exercise a bit of control over recalling past memories, another disturbing situation arose. Within seconds of going within, somewhere on my body there would be an urgent itch that needed scratching. In the beginning I'd attend to that area then try to go back into silence. Realization it was a distraction led me to ignore the physical interference. It eventually stopped happening.

A further developmental stage progressed from remembering past events or thinking of future ones to seeing spheres of colors when my eyes closed. They would come and go changing from one beautiful orb to another. It was like seeing bright colorful balls of energy appear, grow in size and then disappear to transform into a new ball of energy in a different shade. Although aware of them, I concentrated on my breath by counting each exhalation from one to ten and then repeating the process.

With consistent practice, my time of reflection increased to forty-five minutes. Now when my mind emptied, there was mostly blackness. Sometimes it seemed like a dark void and at other times, I'd see a fabric covering. Occasionally a light in the distance would emerge. It would appear as a really small ball of an extremely bright white-yellow light and begin to expand slightly before disappearing.

APARTMENT VISIT

A variety of interesting things happened when I meditated for longer periods of time. (For me that's between forty-five minutes and an hour.) One occurrence surfaced when my daughter moved to an apartment in another state. I envisioned a slide show of the place she was going to occupy. I'd been concerned about the building

59

security and type of area in which it was located. During medita-
tion, I visualized her new neighborhood and apartment complex.

Later that year I had a chance to visit. Getting out of the car, I
looked up at her new home. It was a little different from what I'd
seen during my forty-five minute meditation. The buildings had
colorful geometric patterns on them, but I'd seen a different design
during my short movie clip. My daughter escorted me up to her
apartment and out onto the balcony. From my description of its
arrangement, she immediately understood the view I'd seen came
from looking off her balcony to the building across the street.

I keep a journal nearby where occasionally I'll record an experience
immediately following a session. I've watched several other scenarios
involving people unfold. But, it's usually from the position of an
observer not as a participant.

ENTERING THE VOID

It was early evening around seven o'clock. I assumed my medi-
tative position and set a timer for forty-five minutes. The room was
dimly lit and calm as I mentally prepared myself to go within. On
this particular occasion I slowly became immersed in a deep concen-
trated state of relaxation. No thoughts floated around in my head,
there was just a peaceful attentiveness.

Gradually an awareness came of a physical difference. In fact,
my body felt as if it were dissolving. I couldn't feel flesh, muscles
or bones. My anatomical structure appeared to be evaporating. I
seemed to be entering a space where everything was dark. There was
a complete lack of color. Needless to say, this was totally different
from my usual experiences. I'd sat in one position for close to an
hour feeling no tenseness or soreness in any of my joints. Although
this encounter felt peaceful, it frightened me. I stopped the med-
itation wanting to feel body parts again to assure myself that all
was normal.

A great deal of thought was given to this episode over the years and
what it meant. I now wonder if that's how my body feels when it astral
travels. During sleep when exiting and re-entering our framework do
we have special abilities? Can we subconsciously shut off senses within

our physique when in a meditative state? We've all seen monks and yoga instructors maintain a lotus position for long periods of time and not feel sore or develop arm or leg cramps. Even though distractions such as twitches or the urge to scratch an itch no longer occur, I've not tried to consciously go back in the void. But who knows, I might one day.

DIFFERENT FORMS OF MEDITATION

All meditation sessions should begin by settling in a comfortable position. Place your hands palms up on your knees or in your lap. Relax. Your eyes can be open or closed according to your preference. Focus on your breathing. Begin by placing your tongue behind your upper teeth. Breathe in through your nose to the count of four seconds, hold the breath for the count of four seconds, then breathe out through your mouth to the count of four seconds. Do this three times then return to normal or regular breathing.

There are many ways to meditate. As long as you achieve the inner peace, you may utilize whatever method works for you. Here are some of the various forms available. The key is to be consistent.

SOUND MEDITATION: OMH (AUM OR OM)

Om is a sound that affects brain wave patterns to induce positive effects, including heightened focus. In Hindu, the tenor in 'Omh' creates or symbolizes the vibration of the Universe. Said slowly and correctly it resonates through the abdomen, then the chest, and finally the head.

BREATH

Concentrate on your breath by counting each exhale from one to ten and then begin with one again. The objective is to clear your mind of all chatter during the meditation time. When a thought enters your head, acknowledge it and let it go. Return to counting your breath starting back at one again.

PRAYER

Prayers are a form of meditation. Praying without ceasing can be contemplative, relaxing and healthy for your mind, body and soul. It will assist you in achieving inner peace. Some individuals use rosary beads and others use worry beads during their quieting of the mind.

61

Nature

Walking meditation is very reflective and a way to commune with nature. We had a fish tank when the children were younger. One of the ways my son relaxed after school was sitting and watching fish swim peacefully in a tank full of water. During vacations at the shore, children entertained themselves by jumping waves and playing in the sand. My sister and I sat in beach chairs observing undulating waves transform the oceans panoramic view. We found nature peaceful and calming.

Music

Although most people meditate in silence, my husband has always preferred listening to music. He said jazz erased his mind of all thought. It's another vehicle leading to peace within. Classical music has the same effect on other people.

Mindfulness

It's an act of deep concentration that enables one to achieve focus on being present. It became popularized by Thich Nhat Hahn, a monk from Vietnam who introduced _Mindful Breathing Meditation_ to the Western World.

Meditation is an action. Mindfulness is a state of being. Both are methods of calming and enhancing concentration levels. One focuses on spiritual growth dating from ancient times with the goal of achieving an inner state of peace and serenity. It includes the practice of going within to attain a higher level of consciousness.

The other is the act of truly being one in the present. Insightful awareness of whatever task you're involved in performing. You become mindful by looking deeply into things. For example: if sweeping a floor one must become totally engrossed on everything involved with the task. You notice how the individual strands of the broom sway when moved back and forth, etc. In the act of dining, living in the here and now means whole hearted participation in absorbing the aroma, taste, temperature, colors, etc. of the food.

Mindfulness involves resisting thoughts that intrude in order to remain focused on keeping an awareness on the task you're in the process of completing. Colette Baron-Reid wrote _"Mindfulness is about being observant and remaining neutral."_ Concentration is centered on breathing and quieting the mind comparable to meditation. Both are similar in prioritizing being present. Eyes can be open or closed depending upon personal preference. If sweeping, vision might be a viable option. When eating, whether to open or close them can be a choice.

Living in the present moment means being alert to where you are and what you're doing. As a participant, one is not overly affected by surrounding activity. It can be done anywhere. Most prefer a quiet place where they can close their eyes and focus on their breath. But it can also be practiced when you're caught in stand-still traffic. Observe your thoughts and emotions and let them go without passing judgment.

We're not meditating for the purpose of changing, reforming or correcting anything or anyone. It has nothing to do with a person or a condition. It has to do with realizing a Spiritual Presence within each of us. Once you learn to fully saturate yourself in meditation, you open a doorway to that still small inner voice.

BECOMING PRESENT

Past experiences only come to mind if we recall them. Thoughts about the future often bring anxiety of the unknown. But, by becoming present, a sense of peace will prevail and our bodies will feel lighter.

TRANSCENDENTAL MEDITATION (TM) AND THE MAHARISHI EFFECT

TM refers to a specific type of silent meditation created in Madras, India in 1957. It's a technique practiced for twenty minutes each day while sitting comfortably with eyes closed. In 1960, Maharishi Mahesh Yogi predicted this technique would improve quality of life for the global population. Negative vibrations would be reduced giving rise to peaceful interactions around the world.

Scientific documentation of this phenomenon came in 1976 when practiced in a small community. Crime rate was reduced by 16% on average. In 1978 the Maharishi Global Ideal Society had 108 countries participate in a worldwide TM meditation. The result was growth in harmony and a reduction in crime for all participating sites.

Humans vibration levels can be calibrated as noted in chapter five. Country levels can also be measured using the same technique. The TM method shows the positive benefit of group meditation. When 1% of the world's population regularly practiced transcendental meditation, the overall mood helped repel negativity and led to an increase in peacefulness around the globe.

SUMMARY

All of these techniques require focused attention and consistency. We become observant while experiencing the present moment. Everyone can benefit from these activities. Regularly scheduled ten minute sessions will improve our self-discipline and assist us in letting go of what no longer serves our highest purpose.

Meditation helps us go to peace within. It requires practice and patience. But, the more we reflect the more sensitive we become to what's truly important. In the silent mind, we strive to become an observer, to reach a level of detachment, and eventually to become aware of a higher state of consciousness.

Chapter 16

KUNDALINI RISING

*It's described as a sleeping serpent coiled three and a half
times at the base of your spine.*

Dr. Barbara Condron

Kundalini:
It is a source of energetic power located at the base of the spine.

When released it moves up the spine through the center of the back
to the base of the neck.

It activates in different ways in different individuals.

Release can occur spontaneously or be accelerated with the help
of a healer.

MY KUNDALINI RISING

*Experiencing my Kundalini Rising was electrifying to put it
mildly. It all began one evening while sitting in my den. In my left
ear I heard a voice say, "You're a healer". Reflex action had me
turning to see who was talking and of course no one else was in the
room. Perhaps I'm hearing things or it could've been the person on
television speaking. Yeah, sure I thought when you start hearing
voices, it's definitely time for a break.*

Getting up from my chair, I walked over to the television to shut it off. When I touched the VCR recorder box the TV was sitting on, my fingers felt a sharp electrical jolt. A glance at the recorder, indicated it was now malfunctioning. That jolt had short circuited it. Periodically, I've experienced static electricity in the air and sometimes gotten a little spark. However, the force of the electrical surge really caught me by surprise.

After I calmed down, I tentatively touched the television. Nothing happened that time so it could be turned off. Now there's a minor dilemma because the recorder had only been purchased from a department store a few weeks prior. Since it was no longer working it had to be replaced. Fortunately, I had purchased the insurance warranty.

When I returned the recorder back to the store, there were no clerks in the electronic department. I spent a good ten to fifteen minutes looking for a sales representative. Finally, a manager showed up. Upon seeing me he asked if he could be of assistance. I explained the recorder wasn't operating properly and needed to be exchanged. Without further questions, he simply took the box. A couple of minutes later he came back with a newer edition than the model I was returning and said have a good day.

Zapping the VCR recorder was my initiation into the onset of many short-circuiting incidents. Periodically, I'd get a surge of power that would turn on every light in a room, activate electronic equipment, or make telephones ring in the middle of the night when there was no one on the line.

I searched the internet trying to discover information on what was happening with me. Articles varied with some revealing terrifying examples of people harming themselves. The more I read, the more concerned I became. These minor electrical jolts were happening whenever I touched things around my house.

Many articles identified Kundalini as the source. This was a word I'd never heard of. Seeking more information on the subject, I went to my local book store. After scanning several publications, I purchased Kundalini Rising by Dr. Barbara Condron. The need to learn more about changes taking place within my body was paramount. Her book described my condition as a power surge that rose from the base of the spine up one's back to the base of the neck.

Now that I knew my condition, it became necessary to learn how to control it. Jolts were coming constantly without my seeing a pattern to them. I routinely caused our home security system to malfunction. It was intimidating to even attempt turning light switches on or off.

SHORT CIRCUIT INCIDENTS

This force was something I had to learn to manage or it would control me. My electrical surges were especially effective on my husband's sensitive automobiles. One day while visiting a friend whose husband was having blood circulation issues in his legs, I did a hands-on session to make him more comfortable. Departing to get into my car, my hand reached for the door handle on the driver's side and I heard it zap. I couldn't get into the automobile. Not knowing what to do, I mentally began talking to the car, asking the Angels to please let me get this vehicle home. My friend who had walked out to the curb with me was amused. I could hear her laughter as I finally managed to open the passenger side door and climbed over to get into the driver's seat. Upon arriving home, I explained to my husband there was something wrong with the car. He immediately took it to the dealer's service department. The electrical system had short-circuited.

Another incident occurred when he bought me a beautiful sedan. It had all the bells and whistles one could possibly want. The color was a lovely shade of gray with wooden accessories in the interior and soft cream colored leather seats. I loved the car. One day I went into our garage to drive it to the store. When I touched the car door handle, the trunk flew open, all of the lights came on, the sun roof slid back, the horn started tooting, and all of the doors unlocked. Needless to say, I was not amused. No matter what I tried, I couldn't turn the blaring alarm system off. Not one of the car key functions operated. I had to call my husband to shut it down.

Following that incident, he made sure to purchase a car for me that had no sensitive frills. The only thing the next SUV had was power steering and windows. I even had a situation with that car too.

I took my grandniece for her doctor's appointment and parked in the hospital garage. After her doctor visit was over we came back to the car. I unlocked it with the key, but it wouldn't start. Now here I am in a hospital garage, this child had to go back to school and the car was having fun with me. Making myself calm down I began mentally talking with the car angels about starting this vehicle to get both of us home. It finally started after about ten minutes. Later when I pondered why this happened, I realized that I'd subconsciously activated my kundalini energy in the doctor's office. Before her surgeon entered the room, I'd mentally scanned her body to make sure she got a clean bill of health.

Workshop Classes

Having power surges was troubling. There wasn't a definitive pattern to their occurrence. I also didn't want to electrocute myself accidentally. My daughter suggested learning Reiki, a spiritually guided technique for accessing the body's energy using hands on procedures.

Hospitals in our county send flyers advertising workshops as part of their community outreach program. One happened to come in the mail offering an Alternative Medicine workshop in Reiki Level 1. It would be taught by a certified hospital staff member. I registered to attend. Thus began my involvement in attending workshops to learn more about balancing energy found within my body.

This was the onset of learning about self healing techniques through coincidental encounters with various individuals. One was with a gentleman who approached me at a book store. He initiated a conversation with me. Although I listened attentively, there was still a bit of skepticism. His Father who was accompanying him came over to reinforce the fact that I needed to learn Reiki Energy at a place called Circle of Miracles. This gentleman kept talking with me until I agreed to check it out on the internet. After calling to see the date of their next session, I enrolled for the training to became a Reiki Master Teacher.

A second chance occurrence came in the parking lot at Circle of Miracles. I went to attend a workshop that unknown to me had been canceled. Since I hadn't pre-registered, I wasn't notified. In the parking lot I encountered a lady who came to return a book. We began a conversation during which she suggested I attend Eric Pearl's Reconnection Energy workshop. As fate would have it, the event was being held in our metropolitan area the following weekend. Thinking our meeting was no chance coincidence, I checked the internet and registered to attend. Again, over the course of a couple of years, I became certified as a Level 3 Reconnection Practitioner. The third level is a powerful technique with amazing results. Everyone has a different experience when exposed to it.

A couple of years later while driving to the train station to pick up my daughter from work, she called to let me know she missed her train. The next available one would be in an hour. Since I was almost at the destination, it was easier to go to the nearest book store to wait. As I was browsing the shelves, I caught a book that started to fall. It was Eden Energy Medicine by Donna Eden. When a book literally falls into my hands like this, I assume it's meant for me. After reading the jacket information and being inspired by her experiences, I purchased it. About a month or so later, an email came advertising her workshop sessions. They sounded interesting so I enrolled in the two-year program. This resulted in my certification as an Eden Energy Medicine Practitioner. Energy medicine has been an amazing tool. It taught me how to ground myself.

I attended workshops offering Reiki, the Reconnection, and Eden Energy Medicine. All of these modalities taught that our body is energetic and to remain healthy it was necessary to keep it in balance. But the most important lesson for me was learning how to ground myself and no longer short-circuit electronic equipment. Although, there are still occasions when my inner power structure is elevated and things like my cell phone will not respond or my computer will malfunction. When my energy level appears to be elevating, I wash my hands in cold water, relax and think calming thoughts.

When Divine Source wants you to engage in something pre-destined, all will go smoothly. There is never a glitch. Things seem to flow and it will never cost you to follow in the Universe's planned events. Any monetary expenditures will usually be returned in some manner.

HEALING HANDS HOSPITAL VISIT

My Kundalini energy came in handy when Allison, a young lady, was hospitalized. She had minor surgery that generally necessitated a one night stay in the hospital. Her friend Carol and I sat in the waiting area talking while she was undergoing surgery. At the conclusion of the procedure, the Doctor came to let us know the operation was successful.

She was now in the recovery room. We stayed until she was awake. Both of us wanted to make sure she was comfortably situated in a hospital bed before leaving. Surgery seemed to have gone quite well.

> Later that same evening I received a telephone call. An individual I assumed was a nurse, requested that someone bring Allison's medicine to the hospital. I told my husband that she must be in trouble. We needed to get to her at once. Hospitals don't call and ask for a patient's medicine. They supply everything needed from their pharmacy. Allison was having a serious problem.
>
> When we entered her hospital room, she was attached to several monitors and intravenous tubes. I instinctively touched her forehead. She was burning up with fever. Lowering her temperature was a must. Standing beside her bed, I placed both of my hands on her. As the energy in my hands activated, it short circuited her electronic monitors. When cut off, the monitors would beep. A nurse would then come in and reset the gauges.
>
> I knew my energy was affecting the machinery so I always removed by hands when the nurse came in. After she reset the monitors and left, I replaced them. It was necessary for me to keep my hands on Allison until she cooled. This took about twenty minutes. When my energy is high and healing is occurring, my hands turn a bright red. I kept them on her until my hands returned to their normal color. Now I knew she would be okay. When she closed her eyes falling into a peaceful sleep my husband and I returned home.

The next morning her surgeon wanted to find the source of her fever. Tests conducted showed internal bleeding, but they couldn't discover where it came from. The energy channeled through my hands helped Allison heal the source of her bleeding. One of the interesting things about Divine Universal assistance with healing is that when you heal from within there is no scar tissue. You heal completely. The hospital personnel saw the dried blood from internal bleeding, but couldn't discover the source. The energy had sealed the gap.

HEALING INTERNAL TEAR

> Henry, a young man, passed a kidney stone while at work one morning. He was in severe pain so he went to the hospital. The

medical personnel took blood samples. I'm not sure whether they gave him medicine or not. He called me to say he had a problem and was experiencing lots of pain. I would see him the coming weekend.

When he came, I had him lay down on a massage table. My hand seemed to know where to go for the issue. When I placed my hand on his side he yelped and jumped. The hand had gone right to the affected location. He said my touch felt like a cup of very hot coffee. I suggested he relax and kept my palm and fingers there until I felt coolness. It was only for a couple of minutes or more.

Kundalini energy from my hand went right to the source of his pain and helped him heal it. When activated the electrical source is very powerful. When I touch a person, my hands will turn a bright red if there is an issue of concern. They'll then radiate heat or icy cold depending on what the body needs. And, they instinctively identify where the issue is and go right to it.

MISCELLANEOUS SHORT CIRCUITING

Constantly zapped my iPad by touching it. If left alone and plugged in, it would usually return to default settings. When that didn't work I'd have to take it to be rebooted.

My cell phone had to be carried separately. It couldn't be placed in a pocket or on me at all. I would either drain the batteries or over power them. Fortunately, we have a land line at home.

When visiting my son's family, we sleep in the guest room. My husband said the ceiling light flashed on in the middle of the night waking him. Then it went off.

The mobile phone in the bedroom I used at my sister's house would no longer get a dial tone. It also kept glowing a bright green on and off throughout the night even though it was unplugged. When I left, my sister said it went back to normal working condition.

Four of us had lunch at a friend's home. When time to leave, we stood in a circle holding hands with our eyes closed. One of the participants gave a prayer for all mankind. Suddenly, all of our hands began to slowly rise into the air. When I opened my eyes, everyone was looking at me. I not only caused our hands to rise, I also sent heat into the palms of the people holding my hands on either side of me.

SUMMARY

Energy surges are fascinating. Now, mine are usually harmless and don't cause any massive charges. I've learned to avoid accidentally zapping things by grounding myself. It also helps washing my hands in cold water and going to peace within.

They say there are no coincidences. It's hard to explain, but I felt guided or led to all of the energy workshops I attended. My need was to learn to control this gift of Kundalini energy and to use it only when necessary. I'm not sure how it works. What might happen is that my hands assist the person's body in healing itself. I think the energy activates our ability to go within, something we are all capable of doing.

Chapter 17

HEAL THYSELF

When it comes to healing, perhaps the most important factors are the thoughts in our mind and the emotion in our heart.

Kelly N. Gores

There's an old saying, "You can bring a horse to water, but you can't make him drink." You can open a healing channel from the Divine Source's energy for someone, but you can't make that person accept the healing energy.

The human body is a tremendous piece of machinery. It's made of skin and bones and filled with organs, muscles, tendons and fluid. By itself it can do nothing. It contains a God chip within called the 'Soul'. This chip is said to be located behind an area between our eyes known as the third eye.

Our soul is a master computer. It's artificial intelligence at its' zenith with the ability to operate the body with impunity. It can make the body laugh or cry, walk or become paralyzed, talk or be deaf, have sight or experience blindness, etc.

This life force is the command center whose software is housed in the heart. The heart is the most powerful organ in the body. It's responsible for sending signals to the brain from data received through fluid from other body organs, tissues and muscles. These signals tell the brain what to do, when to do it and how to do it. The soul is a master of pattern development with the ability to learn from repeated functions. In the process of healing, one must be able to tap into this main frame, go within, and commune with the inner self.

"How does one go within?"~ through meditation. When we're young, we heal ourselves automatically. Often times when we fell, got a scratch or cut we forgot about it and it healed. Mommy or daddy kissed the hurt, telling us it's okay and instant healing takes place. But as we age and get further away from our birthing origins, there's a tendency to forget those things we instinctively knew as a child.

I don't know if everything can be patched up or fixed. There are people born with pre-existing conditions such as blindness, deafness, and challenging motor skills to name a few. Some afflictions might be karmic, fate or destiny experiences we're meant to have. The question becomes whether these issues are for the person born with the challenge or for someone else? It could be for the family they're born into. For example, learning to work with your handicapped child requires developing great patience and understanding. Having a handicap requires acceptances for and surrendering to learning survival skills. We see instances of this in athletes overcoming great physical challenges caused by injuries or accidents. Through determination, hard work and will power, they learn to overcome them.

WRIST FRACTURE

Years ago as I was leaving my beautician's establishment, I tripped on a cracked curb, fell on my right side and felt a sharp pain. I sat up and looked over my body to see what damage had been done. My legs and feet looked fine so I started to get up and automatically used my hands for assistance. Suddenly an unbearable pain shot up my right arm. I knew I had broken something. A close examination of my arm showed several bones protruding out of place.

Well I thought, it could have been worst. I needed to get home. Since my driving hand was injured, I drove through early morning rush hour traffic using my left one. This was fine until I arrived at my driveway. No way could I park this car in the garage. I drove down the driveway, got out of the car, went into the house and told my husband I thought I'd broken my wrist.

Following the accident, I was so concerned with getting safely home that I ignored any discomfort in my right hand and wrist. Later when thoughts about my accident arose, came the realization I was blessed not to have broken my hip or had a concussion. Relief that only my wrist was injured, resulted in eliminating the pain.

Fast forward: With skillful knowledge of sports injuries, a great Orthopedic Specialist put all my bones back where they belonged. When the operation was over, my wrist was placed in a soft cast. This immobilized it, but allowed flexibility to move my fingers. Of course there was also the recommendation for ten sessions of physical therapy.

Knowing that I needed to help heal myself, I began massaging the area above and below my surgical scar with a healing oil. It was one I made from olive oil and dried herbs. This was applied for fifteen minutes twice a day along with use of a heating pad. I mentally encouraged my wrist to heal through meditation. Every morning I would go into stillness and thank my inner self for healing.

I signed up for physical therapy and began my sessions. At the conclusion of my second appointed visit, the physical therapist said I didn't need the other eight sessions. Healing had occurred quickly. My wrist repaired so completely that within a couple of months I was able to go back to league bowling. If you look at the injured area today, you would never know it was ever broken. The surgical stitches were placed in such a manner they look like a vein, not a scar.

In conversation with my sister who was a nurse, I mentioned having no pain from the accident. She said the nerves in my hand must have been damaged. That bothered me so I stuck myself with a needle and instantly felt pain. No nerve damage had occurred. That's when I realized that a person could possibly control the level of pain experienced.

BURNT HAND

The second healing incident occurred several years ago. My husband was cooking dinner at the stove with my niece standing next to him watching. I walked up to them and immediately placed my right hand on a hot electric burner. I was stunned and wondered what in the world just happened. Instantly, my hand turned bright red, was quite painful and extremely hot. I immediately placed it under cold running water in the sink to cool it down. This of course did not work.

After years of dealing with intense migraines and a broken wrist, I'd learned to ignore or control my pain response. My concern focused on soothing the burn. I was afraid my hand was going to be one giant blister. I got an ice pack out of the freezer to try to cool it down. That wasn't working. My hand was so hot it melted the ice packs as quickly as they were put on. During the same time, I'm telling myself "you're a healer so you should be able to heal this hand".

My niece who had worked in a doctor's office for several years, told me to go to the hospital because this was a major burn. But I kept thinking this burn was some kind of test from the Universe. Under normal circumstances, I'd never ever put my entire hand, fingers as well as the palm, on a hot burner. I kept mentally telling my hand it had to heal itself. At the same time, I tried everything I could think of to cool it down while continuing to apply ice. My palm was bright red, but it hadn't blistered yet.

Over the next three to four hours I tried a variety of ointments for burns with no luck. Finally, I called my sister and asked what our Mother used for burns in the olden days. She told me Toots used baking soda. There was a box of baking soda in the spice cabinet. I retrieved it and sprinkled some on my hand. It didn't work. But I was still drawn to baking soda. Suddenly I recalled having some in the basement pantry.

About a month before this incident, we purchased a large bag of baking soda from super grocery market. My husband asked me why I was buying such a large quantity because we would never need it based on the amount of cooking we did. I told him I'd probably use it in my bath water for a good relaxing soak.

I quickly went down to the pantry and got it. After cutting the top off, I placed my hand directly into the bag. Instantly the burn began to cool. My hand was wet from holding constantly melting ice cubes. When I dipped my hand into the bag, it made a paste over my entire palm and fingers. Within less than a half-hour, my hand looked perfectly normal. You'd never know it had been burnt. Curiosity made me wonder why the box of baking soda in my spice *cabinet wasn't effective? The box information said it was refined. Thank goodness the large bag contents weren't. As a precaution, I slept with baking soda paste on my hand covered with a plastic glove.*

Normally, if I were testing something hot, I'd wet a finger before touching. This was my entire hand, palm and all of the fingers. What was the purpose? Then of course, I knew I had to heal myself. So, for the next four hours it took from the initial burning to the baking soda application, every thought in my head was set on figuring out how to heal myself. Once again, pain became a choice. I was so intent on wondering why I'd placed my entire hand on a hot burner and how to cure it that I felt no pain.

Two weeks later, small white patches appeared on my palm. As they came, I removed them. My hand peeled in small patches until all of the affected skin had been removed. It was amazing. Even this occurred with a witness. I was visiting a friend from one of my Eden Energy classes at the time the skin began to peel away. It started as a tiny patch on my palm and as each patch was removed another one began until my entire hand had all of the old skin peeled away. Within two days my palm and fingers looked exactly the same as they had before the burn episode.

Although my hand was burnt and hot enough to melt ice instantly, it never blistered. But the damaged skin had to be replaced. I assume this is why the patches appeared. They were removing all of the destroyed skin tissues from that four hour ordeal.

POST SCRIPT:

A week later while using an old paper cutter at the church office where I volunteered, I accidentally cut a finger on the same hand. Because it was a deep cut, it bled profusely. My concern was not only the laceration but also the fact it was a rusty piece of equipment. I visited an Urgent Care facility on the way home. The doctor stitched the finger. He also gave me a tetanus booster shot since my last remembered one was over ten years prior.

Later, I surmised the finger cut occurred to make me get a booster shot. My system needed the protection because the burn had been so severe. The finger healed so well you won't find that cut either. When the Universe tested me, it made sure I had what I needed to heal myself in advance. It also supplied two witnesses to the burn and one to the peeling away of the injured skin. Without witnesses to this burning experience, I'd have thought I dreamt it.

Was this a lesson from the Universe reinforcing human's innate ability to go within for healing? For four hours I tolerated an extremely hot burnt hand. But it didn't blister. There's no logical explanation for this encounter. I'm not sure if I felt pain and just ignored it or that my psyche didn't allow my body to experience it. The level of suffering experienced become a choice.

Healing is a process. Sometimes we feel guilty that we are here and healthy while others are less fortunate. But, we have to remember that we are simply a drop of water in the vast ocean called life. There's still a lot we don't know. No matter what your condition is physically, emotionally or mentally, how you handle the situation is more important than the condition. It's what makes you who you become.

INITIATION

According to Norma Milanovich & Shirley McCune, authors of the book: <u>Light Shall Set You Free</u>", levels of initiation are tests that all spiritual seekers must complete on their journey. These trials are designed to strengthen the body while facilitating change within. One of the conditions for passing the tests is ultimately, self-control over one's mental and emotional bodies. Tests include:

- Speaking one's truth
- Understanding of Universal Laws *(see Appendix E)*
- Learning unconditional love
- Serving humanity
- Seeing inter-dimensionally
- Enlightenment

Chapter 18

EMPATHY

An Empath is someone born with the innate ability to feel and understand what other people (as well as other living things such as animals and in some cases even plants) are feeling and experiencing.

Sydney Campos

Empathy is the experience of connecting one's energy with another person both physically and emotionally. Being an empath is not something I consciously intended to become. It just happened, especially with family members and close friends. Conversing with someone who had an ache or pain could result, by the end of our conversation, with that person being fine and me experiencing the ache or pain. Consciously or sub-consciously I then go within to heal the concern. Apparently it's been a life long habit. My eldest sister often reminded me to be careful. She knew it was instinctively done.

Normally, it's a minor issue like lowering someone's blood pressure or taking away a headache. One day I was talking with a friend on the telephone who said she had a stomach problem. By the end of our conversation she was fine and I had an upset stomach that I then had to heal. But in all of the empathic occurrences, I knew relatively quickly whose health concern I was taking on.

Asthma Attack

One particular incident involving an asthma attack was fascinating. It occurred when Agnes, was experiencing tachycardia and lung health concerns. She was in and out of the hospital emergency rooms because of experiencing cardiac rapid pulsations as well as asthmatic breathing problems. Visits with both a Cardiologist and a Pulmonary Specialist were almost on a monthly basis.

She lived alone and had a multitude of physical concerns to deal with. I tended to astral travel at night to make sure she was okay. Apparently, this was one of those occasions. Agnes was having both an asthma attack as well as arrhythmia. Thinking her body couldn't handle both the lung and the heart issue at the same time, I consciously decided to intervene. If I took on the respiratory problem, she could deal with the coronary one.

It was absolutely amazing to experience an asthma attack. For years, I'd suggested that when she felt an attack coming on not to panic, to remain calm and take a deep breath from the bottom of her lungs; that she should concentrate on inhaling and exhaling from her abdomen. Easy for me to say, but not for a person having an attack.

When I awoke from that astral travel experience, I thought what a joke! While experiencing her asthma attack, I remember saying to myself, *"Good grief, you really can't breathe"*. Fortunately, I was observing myself having the attack, not participating in the reality of it. For a person having an asthmatic incident, it can be a very frightening feeling. Many people die because they can't catch their breath. I now have much respect for asthma sufferers.

Heart Attack

Another empathic incident involved my heart.

It was a warm sunny day in August. Agnes and I were in a parking lot at the local shopping mall when suddenly there was pounding in my chest area. It was an unusual occurrence so my first inclination was to determine why I was having this issue. To the best of my knowledge, my body was in good condition. Agnes was the one with cardiac issues, but she was with me and it wasn't her. The attack was thought provoking. I was at peace within myself and not doing anything physically strenuous. There was no reasonable explanation for this incident. The fluttering lasted for what seemed like minutes because of their intensity, but was probably only seconds. They ceased and we continued shopping.

Assuming this was not my affliction, I wondered whose palpitations they were. That evening, I called family members asking if anyone was having health concerns. Everyone said they were fine. There was no sense in worrying about the situation. If it was a serious complaint, the throbbing would come again.

This throbbing came on and off for several months. There was no discernible pattern to them and could happen at any time day or evening. They came when I was going up or down stairs, walking or just sitting in a chair. After each occurrence, I would massage my upper chest area to relax it still reflecting upon whose coronary concerns these were. At no time did I ever think they were mine.

Things took a dramatic turn about six months after experiencing that first rapid heart beat situation. It was winter season. That particular day the temperature fell below thirty degrees and we got eight inches of snow. I went outdoors to help clear our driveway. Shoveling snow was something I enjoyed doing. It was my winter exercise. Since our driveway slants down, I always start removing snow at the top and my husband would use the snow-blower starting at the bottom.

After removing five or six shovels of snow, the tremors began. I promptly ceased and stood still but they continued. Suddenly I experienced the most excruciating pains in my upper chest region. They were so intense, it took my breath away. Retreating into the house, I began massaging the heart area trying to calm it.

My stomach began to churn and I knew regurgitation was imminent. Racing to the bathroom I made it in the nick of time for everything eaten that day to heave itself into the toilet bowl. At the same time, I was in agony and needed to lie down. This felt like an actual heart attack.

Massaging my chest area was not having any effect. Contemplating how to calm it down I thought perhaps using a crystal to absorb the pain might work. Going upstairs to my den *where several of them are kept, I selected a large clear quartz crystal. Cradling the crystal on my chest, I laid down on the sleep sofa and closed my eyes. Approximately ten minutes or so later the pain vanished. The quartz that had felt ice cold when placed on my upper torso, was now extremely hot. I rinsed it under cool tap water, dried it off and replaced it back onto the bookcase shelf. Since the pain and palpitations had subsided, I now felt fine as if the incident hadn't occurred. Without further deliberation, I went back outdoors and continued shoveling snow.*

Later that same evening I called relatives and close friends and asked if anyone was experiencing health issues. Once again all said they were fine. I knew intuitively this was not my problem and that it belonged to someone else. The question was who?

Things came to an abrupt halt four days later on Palm Sunday. I'd gone to my church's early Morning Prayer Service. On the way home, I decided to attend my niece's church service in an adjacent state. This was something I routinely did to show support for her ministry. As I was driving, the tachycardia attack proceeded to emerge again. Now picture this, I'm on a major three-lane highway going at least sixty miles an hour. I knew I couldn't handle sharp chest pain and drive. As the distress slowly continued to intensify, I immediately said out loud with conviction. "I will not accept you, go back where you came from". The pain instantly subsided and I continued on my way with no further complications.

Two o'clock in the afternoon, I returned home from a most inspirational worship service with my niece and her congregation. A telephone call had come from Gregory. His wife, Yvette, was in the hospital. She too had gone to an early prayer service that morning. Afterwards as she drove onto her driveway, the attack hit. Yvette had severe chest pains and vomiting. It was a repeat of what I'd experienced earlier in the week. Gregory immediately took her to the local hospital emergency room. Following an examination, the doctor felt she should be admitted. Later that same evening, she was transferred to a top cardiac facility. Two days later, she had triple bi-pass surgery.

Until that telephone call, I had no clue whose cardiac condition was being experienced. Usually issues were mostly as an observer watching myself heal them. But this experience of having someone else's actual attack had reached a new plateau. It meant participation in real time. Did this mean the symptoms felt were all in the mental and emotional realm, not physical?

Having this circumstance continue over many months was a bit traumatic. Normally an ailment will come and go within a day or two, a week at the most. Because of the intensity and duration of this experience, it was important to discover if I had physically damaged my heart as well. An appointment with my primary physician to get a complete check-up including an EKG exam showed all was fine. I got a clean bill of health from both my medical doctor and a Cardiologist. When the Radiologist was performing a scan, I managed to view a picture of my heart beating. No damage had been done during this episode.

Fast Forward Repetition

Several months later the rapid pounding began again. Immediately I thought it must be Yvette so I telephoned to find out how things were progressing. Was she still under her doctor's care? When was her last visit and how was she feeling now? She said occasionally she had problems breathing and felt quickening pulsations. In an effort to get to the root cause of this, I asked her to keep a log. In it she was to record the date and time of palpitations, and what was happening. Was she walking, talking on the telephone, etc. I asked her to document this information for a couple of weeks.

Compiling this data displayed a picture of the cause for her health concerns. Skipping beats intensified whenever she was dealing with one particular stressful situation. This was an eye opener for her. (*Often just knowing the cause can help eliminate the problem*). Stress can and will manifest into a variety of physical illnesses. Yvette realized she had to surrender to what is. Acceptance of what she could and couldn't do when other people were involved, was the key to alleviating her illness.

Upon reflection, automatically assuming symptoms from others came with the following conclusion. It depends on our relationship. If it's one of my children, a close friend, or relative I subconsciously feel their pain. If it's something I can assist them with, it's automatically done without conscious thought. This particular incidence let me know that if the burden is too much for me to bear, I can send it back to the originating owner. The heart attack situation was a real wake up call. I couldn't heal the problem. I just delayed Yvette doing so herself. But perhaps it was postponed until all was in place for her successful operation and outcome.

Heart Massaging Dream

While on a tour of the Finger Lakes later that summer, I again experienced rapid pulsations. They came and left quickly. Two days later they occurred again lasting for a few seconds even though it felt like several minutes. I wondered whose palpitations they were. I knew my heart was fine having taken an EKG and Radiologist scan at the Cardiologist's office earlier that summer. My body was in good condition, so whose cardiac ordeal was this. Yvette instantly came to mind, but after triple bi-pass surgery, she should have been fine.

Throbbing happened again three days later in the early evening. It would occur out of the blue at any time whether sitting, walking, eating, etc. Since they belonged to someone else, I had no control over their timing.

That night in a dream state, my palms and fingers were viewed cradling a heart organ. It was situated in my hands and not attached to any part of the body. In the vision, my thumbs were gently massaging it. Looking at the clock when I momentarily awoke showed hands around two a.m. Acknowledging the time, I succumbed back to sleep. While getting dressed in the morning, I recalled the dream. Whose heart had I soothed during the night?

I talked with Yvette later in the evening. During our conversation when asked if she'd been tired lately or having any health concerns, her immediate response was no all was fine. But after some thought, she mentioned waking up during the night having trouble breathing. At first she couldn't catch her breath. But then after realizing a sense of relief, she returned right back to sleep and woke up feeling great the next morning. I asked her if she recalled what time it happened. She said around two o'clock. Was it her organ I'd tweaked during the night? Who knows?

Summary

Learning to avoid taking on other people's health issues in order to heal them is not easy. It's instinctive sub-conscious behavior and not something knowingly done. _Oneness,_ _by Rashi,_ contains a chapter discussing life's repeating patterns. Empathy was one of mine. But, I had a rude awakening. Experiencing the asthma attack wasn't too bad, but having someone else's heart attack raised this repeating pattern to a new level. Becoming aware of my habit of accepting other peoples health issues allowed me to let it go. Now if I sub-consciously take on someone's ailment, when I become aware of doing so it's usually returned to the originating owner.

Chapter 19

CHAKRA SYSTEM

Chakras are energy centers in our bodies that, when perceived by those of us who are blessed to be able to see them, look like wheels of light spinning in and around the body–stars in miniature.

Cyndi Dale

Some cultures around the world believe human beings are born with two bodies, a physical one and one composed of pure energy. They consider our inner framework more energetic than solid with Chakras viewed as a vital component of this physique.

The name Chakra is an Indian Sanskrit word meaning wheel or turning. They are said to be power centers that keep the body healthy by recycling energies and balancing them. Alternative healing techniques such as Reiki, and Qi gong, rely on the body's chakra system. When balanced, the body is spiritually, emotionally and physically in harmony. If imbalanced, illness and dis-ease can and often will occur.

There are lots of swirling energy cells in our body. *Sir John Woodroofe in his book The Serpent Power,* focused attention on seven major ones located from the coccyx to the top of our head. These are said to be in alignment with the spinal column as they rise upward toward our crown. Minor chakras are found on the soles of our feet, the palms of our hands, our ears, and various areas throughout our entire mass.

I've often wondered about the chakras in the palm of my hands. When doing a session on someone and my hands turn red, it's a signal that healing is occurring. The individual being touched can feel heat, ice cold, or absolutely nothing. Hands are kept on the area until I intuitively sense it's okay to remove them. It could be a minute or five minutes every situation is different.

Pain tends to radiate. Often the location where the person feels discomfort is not necessarily the area of major concern. My hands, which are usually cold, gravitate to the heat signal sent by the brain. It will activate the palm chakras. When touched, the person will either feel hot or cold, whichever healing temperature the body requires.

Chakras are said to be databases that help us process information from the cells within our body. If you want to heal yourself of any kind of ailment whether it's physical, emotional or spiritual, your chakra system can be the key. Learning more about each of these seven major centers will enable you to target those sources of energy and use them to your advantage.

Experiences are lessons that can have a positive or negative side. We can choose to look at either one or both. To create harmony within our surroundings and ourselves, we look on the favorable side of events and people. This promotes the free flow of energy throughout our system leading us to become healthier, more loving and more spiritual. If we attach negative values to situations, another person or ourselves, it's also recorded in our cellular memory. This impedes the free flow of our life force energy or chi within the body's system. Illness can and will develop if the chakras are imbalanced.

That being said, realize that every thought, every feeling, every memory we've ever had is considered to be retained within our cells. Chakras are able to translate feelings and perceptions from those cellular memories. Let go of thoughts or feelings that drain your power especially from the past. This can be accomplished by talking about them or writing in a journal. As you cleanse yourself, you are committing to live in the present and look to the future.

Chakra Database Recall

Occasionally when hands are placed to rebalance a person's energy, I will intuit a message from the chakra that is involved. A case in particular involved a young lady who came to visit. She was upset because she'd just lost her job and her fiancé changed his mind about getting married. Anger at both her employer for down-sizing and her fiancé for calling off their wedding was quite evident.

During the session I suddenly intuited that neither of them was the issue. From her database chakra information, came the impression she was upset with God. At the end of our session, I asked her. She thought about the question and said yes, she was. God had abandoned her. Instead of being financially independent and becoming a wife she was returning home to live with parents.

Sometimes, just knowing the cause of energy imbalance within a chakra, helps a person to heal. This young lady's experience with both the job and the young man might have been a lesson from the Universe to further her growth in consciousness.

THE MAJOR CHAKRAS

Each of the seven major chakras has a different function and governs a separate location. It will record specific types of data for that particular area. For instance, experiences concerning our self esteem are stored in the third chakra called the Solar Plexus. Experiences concerning our birth family and tribal organizations are retained in our Root Chakra.

By knowing what parts of our anatomy chakras govern, you'll see patterns in your life relating to them. Sometimes you can tell which chakra is involved by your common expressions. Example: He knocks me off my feet (*root chakra, foundation feels unbalanced*); She's a pain in the neck (*throat chakra*).

When balanced, the body's in reasonably good health. If one or more energy centers are blocked, you might feel lethargic, fatigued and blocked creatively. Feelings of fear and worry might also arise. You can do a clearing to assist in balancing these energetic imbalances. The best thing about chakra clearing is its flexibility. Choose the method that feels comfortable for you.

Here is a list of the seven major chakras. Each one has a dominant reference color (*some people might see a different color*). The location and organ it governs as well as some basics is included. Chakras go through the body so the area governed is the same whether in the back or the front.

Root Chakra:

- Color–red
- Location–base of the spine
- It connects us to our parents, family relationships and tribal traditions. Survival instincts of wants and needs.

Sacral Chakra:

- Color–orange
- Location–pelvic bone area, below the navel
- It deals with sexuality and financial relationships as well as creativity, money, power and guilt.

Solar Plexus Chakra:

- Color–yellow
- Location–above the naval
- It relates to our self-confidence, personal power, authority, shame and trust. It has to do with peer pressure and allowing others to define us as opposed to being confident in our self.

Heart Chakra:

- Color–green
- Location–center of the chest (next to your physical heart)
- This chakra deals with forgiveness and surrender. It's related to one's ability to give and receive unconditional love, not the romantic kind often depicted with the heart symbol.

Throat Chakra:

- Color–blue
- Location–hollow of the throat area
- It governs communication, truth and lies, responsibility and will power. This chakra is about speaking your truth.

Brow Chakra:

- Color–indigo
- Location–between the eyes

- It governs our sight and insight, intellect, intuition, illusions and reason. It can be further developed through yoga and martial arts.

CROWN CHAKRA:

- Color–purple
- Location–top of the head
- It connects us to the Divine Source's energy. Positive thoughts, divine guidance and trust affect it. Meditation and prayer can bring a sense of inner peace.

The chakra system is really fascinating. Knowing an illness location can assist you in balancing the chakra involved. Rebalancing it might help eliminate the problem. All of us have the ability to go within and help heal ourselves. At the same time, we're here to experience life. If it's meant for us to have an illness, we will. But, keep in mind that acceptance of a situation, unconditional love and forgiveness are the greatest healers.

Part 3

Chapter 20

GRAVITY CONTROL / DIVINE INTERVENTION

"What goes up must come down."

1st line of a song by David Clayton-Thomas

Gravity comes from the Latin word gravitas meaning heaviness or weight. It deals with mass. Without it, things not attached to the earth in some manner, might float off into space. We are blessed to have it.

Universal Laws rarely change while theories change frequently as new evidence is discovered. Isaac Newton's Law of Gravity describes this as an attraction between two objects. He recounts one of the most common examples of this as an apple falling from a tree. Albert Einstein's Theory of Gravitational Relativity expresses it as a curvature of time and space caused by mass and energy. (*Wikipedia*)

We're exposed to it being manipulated every day. When the Wright brothers flew the first airplane, they managed to control gravity. They used fuel to force their experimental airplane upward to defy the gravitational pull of Earth soaring into the air. Today the aviation industry manipulates gravity on a routine basis to such an extent, that we don't think about the displacement.

In the 1960's, NASA used the mathematical calculations of Katherine Johnson, a young African American employee, to manipulate the Earth's gravitational heaviness to propel a rocket into space. Her calculations assisted Astronaut Glenn Armstrong in guiding his space craft into space to orbit around our planet. She also calculated the safe return of Glenn and his crew back to ground level. With the use of fuel and rocket engineering, humans are capable of defying Earth's gravitational pull.

In his book _The Magic of Believing_, Claude M. Bristol says man through his mind can shape events and control matter. We see examples of this happening in several countries. Developing mind control in people like Indian Guru's assists them in levitating. They can control gravity during a deep concentrated meditation raising their bodies above the ground. The Bible tells us Jesus walked on water and so did his Disciple Peter. (*Matt 14:22-33*)

DIVINE INTERVENTION

My elderly uncle was in the local hospital. He was being discharged into my care the next day. Because of his condition, he couldn't go up and down steps. His home was not equipped with a stair glide so the social worker at the hospital arranged for a hospital bed to be delivered during the afternoon. This meant I had to rearrange the furniture in his dining room to accommodate it.

His row house dining room was small and filled with furniture. There was the table with six chairs. A china closet was filled with gold rimmed plates and crystal stemware. Two smaller cabinets had hurricane lamps and breakable pieces of pottery on and in them. All of the furniture was constructed of heavy wood. I had difficulty moving even one of the dining room chairs. I wasn't sure how I was going to rearrange this place to accommodate a hospital bed by myself. I'd asked around for help but everyone had something to do. The bed would be delivered in an hour. This furniture had to be moved and I needed to find a method of doing so.

As I stood in the archway between the living room and the dining room, I tried to figure out a way to do this. Space had to be provided for the hospital bed that was coming. In desperation, I looked up to the heavens and asked for help. I said, "Holy Angels I need help".

Jesus said: *Ask and it will be given you. Matt 7:7*

When people tell tales about things happening beyond belief, believe them. I asked for help and the most miraculous thing occurred. When I attempted to move a chair, it floated. I was so surprised that I tentatively put my hand back on it. Again when touched, it moved easily. It was as if the chair were weightless. I took this as a sign the Divine Source was giving me the help I asked for.

Every piece of furniture floated when I touched it. The extremely heavy dining room table just slid. His cabinet full of china and crystal moved with a mere touch of my hand. Within a short period of time, all of this heavy mahogany wooden furniture was moved to transform the dining room into a space that would accommodate my uncle's hospital bed.

Satisfied with the room arrangement, I placed my hands in a prayer mode at my heart level and said, "Thank you Holy Angels" and bowed to my Divine assistants.

This was a small miracle. I thought about the many small miracles that happen all over the world. We often read about people who in the case of emergency can seem to develop super human strength, such as a Mother who can lift a car off her small child. Something she could not do under ordinary circumstances. I could never have moved that heavy furniture and cabinet full of dishes and glassware without help from heaven. But it didn't require strength on my part. The pieces just glided when I touched them.

> *Truly I tell you, if you have faith as small as a mus-*
> *tard seed,*
> *you can say to this mountain, "Move from here to there,*
> *and it will move".*
> *Nothing will be impossible for you. Matt 17:20 (NIV)*

I thought there's no way this furniture could have been rearranged without Divine assistance. But, having heard Nassim Haramen from *Resonance Science Foundation* talk about gravity, made me wonder if I went within myself. Did a portal found in all of our bodies open to allow me ability to control or manipulate gravity to move the furniture. I've never done it again, but I haven't needed to.

In her book _Initiation_, Elisabeth Haich offers this insight. *"When an invisible force radiating from the Solar Plexus, can grow to a giant strength; when the person concerned really wants something with all his heart. It can conquer the gravitational pull of the earth"*.

It makes you realize there's a lot yet to learn about life here on Planet Earth and what we as humans inhabiting it are capable of achieving.

Chapter 21

UFO Sightings

Ezekiel saw what is described as a metallic object arriving from the sky that looked like a wheel within a wheel.

Zechariah saw a flying scroll whose measurements he said were 20 cubits by 10 cubits.

Ezekiel 10:9 / Zechariah 5:1

It was nearing lunchtime when I decided to go to the grocery store. What a beautiful sunny day. No chance of rain. Since early childhood, I've always enjoyed looking at the sky when outside or traveling in a car. I love seeing cloud formations and the colors formed by the sun's interaction with them. Atmospheric changes at sunrise, sunset, when storms are coming, etc. are quite colorful.

After driving a half block from home, I happened to look out the car window. To my amazement there was a huge airship in the sky. Stopping my car and getting out was necessary to actually get a better look at what seemed like a large flying chocolate brown triangle. Staring at its shape brought an awareness the airplane had no points. All of the angles were rounded. What a large beautiful structure. Gazing up at it, I realized it made no sound. It also cast no shadow. Had I not looked up into the sky, I'd never have seen it. The object that I thought was a new type of airplane design seemed to hover over the area, moving at a really slow pace. This was a kind of aircraft I'd never seen before.

It was coming from the northwest and going east. I assumed it was traveling to the local Air Force Base. An air show was scheduled to take place that weekend. It was to be their last one because the base was scheduled to close.

I took for granted that this was a new prototype the military had designed. Curiously looking up at the triangular object, I couldn't locate landing gear slots. The underbelly of the craft was seamless and smooth. Of course this made me wonder how it would land and where the openings for the wheel chambers were.

The hovering airship was moving so slowly it appeared to almost stop. After another searching look, I got back into my car and continued driving to the store. When I got to the corner and looked back to see the aircraft, it was gone. It sped away quickly. Again it made no sound, cast no shadow and moved with almost instantaneous speed. I thought this was an amazing new piece of equipment for our Air Force.

Later after arriving back home, I telephoned my son letting him know about this aircraft. I just concluded it was the Stealth Bomber, a relatively new type of airplane design that I had heard so much about, taking part in the Air Show that weekend. Newspaper articles mentioned the Stealth Bomber was quiet and cast no shadow to avoid radar.

My guess the Stealth airplane was what I'd seen prevailed for several years. One evening I watched a documentary on UFO sightings. People in a nearby county were interviewed. They described viewing a large brown triangular shaped object in the sky similar to the one I'd seen that very same day. My curiosity had me accessing my computer. I researched the Stealth Bomber airplane. Of course it looked totally different from the vehicle that flew over my neighborhood. That's when I realized the aircraft was probably a UFO. And, it also explained the speed with which it disappeared.

Meditation Retreat

In the fall that year, I attended a Meditation Retreat. There were several workshops, one of which was given by a UFO buff. When asked if any of us had ever seen a UFO, I spoke up and described it to the group. The workshop leader got really excited and said he had a picture of it to show me.

One of the participants in the group asked if I were scared. To be perfectly honest, it never crossed my mind to have any fear or anxiety. First of all, most people who see UFO's describe them as silver and round. The object in the sky I'd witnessed was chocolate brown and triangular shaped. I was too busy trying to figure out how it was going to land to be afraid. The bottom was smooth and appeared to have no seam lines in it, so where was the landing gear?

The assumption on my part was this plane's participation in the Air Force Base final air show. And now that I think about it, it probably was but as an observer not a participant. One thing about a sighting like this, you don't forget it. It becomes ingrained in your memory bank. There are many unexplainable events occurring around the world. The UFO experience was one I just accepted and moved on.

Kelly's UFO Sighting

My husband and I were vacationing on the Outer Banks of North Carolina in July of 2013. The weather was beautiful. Days were hot and the evenings were a little cooler. The house we were renting with other family members was right off the bay and a half block from the ocean.

I was sitting on the upper deck of a three story house looking out over the water and admiring the stars on this clear night. Where I live we don't often get to see all of the stars because of the light glare from buildings in the surrounding area.

Off in the distance something suddenly appeared in the sky. It seemed to come out of nowhere. It looked to be a round object surrounded by twinkling lights. I wondered to myself if it was a UFO because it had appeared so quickly. I got so excited. I couldn't believe what I was seeing. I wanted to share this sighting with someone, but no one else was around. I knew if I went to find someone to share this with it would be gone before I returned.

The sighting only lasted a few minutes or so even though it seemed longer. The object left as quickly as it came. One second it was there and next it was gone. I was in a state of amazement sitting there staring at the sky for a long while, hoping it would reappear. Knowing that no one would believe me if I told them, I didn't.

Chapter 22

DIMENSIONS

"We live simultaneously in more than one world. We experience space/time coordinates in the physical dimensions, and are bound by space-less/time-less ones in other dimensions.

Norma Milanovich & Shirley McCune

There are many things about life that are fascinating. One of them involves dimensions. Science can't be absolutely certain how many dimensions we have here on Earth. In the past, we tended to view everything as being in the first three dimensions.

- First dimensional space is where a point can be defined by a single number like on a number line.
- Second dimensional space is defined by two points e.g. length and width.
- Third dimensional space has length, width and height. It also has solid mass or form and occupies space.
- Fourth dimensional space adds an element of time
- Fifth dimensional space transcends time and space.

Humans have lived and worked in the third dimension. It's where we receive sensory information through our five senses of sight, taste, hearing, smell and touch.

Occasionally, situations occur that blur the lines between dimensions. Time and space can be relative. Have you ever driven down a major highway and felt a shift in the timing and speed of your vehicle. In some spots, sixty miles an hour seems slow and at other spots that same sixty miles an hour can seem like speeding. I'm not sure if this occurs because of the air current patterns in certain areas or if it's a space time shift. Occasionally, time seems to speed by and other moments, time seems to move very slowly. The following episodes are examples of this blurring between dimensions.

INVISIBLE

On a peaceful relaxing Sunday afternoon, I felt the need to go to a store in a nearby shopping area. When I told my husband, he decided to accompany me since there were no sport games being televised at that time.

There was nothing I really needed, so I wondered why this urgent feeling to go into this particular department store. My husband said he was going to look in the men's department. I strolled around various sections, just looking at but not really interested in any particular items. There were several other customers.

One lady was standing near the women's clothing aisle. I hadn't planned to say anything as I walked past her. But when she looked at me, I could see the misery in her facial expression. I smiled, said hello then asked why she was so sad. That question opened a flood gate response. She began talking about her young adult son who was going through a very trying time. She was quite worried about him and concerned that he was considering suicide. Her entire body reflected the pain she was experiencing. This was her only child and like a lot of parents, she didn't know how to help him and make him understand all was going to be okay.

We talked. I told her that God knew her heart and to give her son into His care. She cried as I hugged her trying to soothe the pain. Fear for her child was all consuming. Unburdening herself seemed to help. We remained like this for what I thought was only a short while with me listening while she talked. Later I found out this conversation took about forty-five minutes. By the time we parted, she appeared to feel calmer. The problem wasn't solved, but she had been given a chance to talk and pour out her anxiety to a sympathetic listener.

Many parents, myself included, wish we could protect our children from unhappy situations. But, everyone is here on Planet Earth to have experiences and to learn from them. Just as our parents tried to shield us from disastrous situations, we do the same things with our children.

My husband saw me standing in the aisle and came over. He wanted to know where I had been and proceeded to complain that he'd been looking for me for almost an hour. Not only had he searched the entire store, he'd even gone outside looking in other stores too. When told him I'd been in the exact same spot the entire time I was in the store, he really looked skeptical.

Suddenly I understood. The Universe sent me to the store to assist that lady. Our entire encounter was invisible to anyone in the third dimension. Didn't Albert Einstein say time and space are relative?

CODE BLUE EPISODE

Allison was taken to the hospital emergency room by a friend. At the time she was experiencing respiratory issues as well as erratic heart impulse concerns. By the time I arrived, she had been placed in an emergency room cubicle with several cords attached to her body monitoring the lungs, heart, and blood pressure.

As I looked at the lung monitor, occasionally a bell would ring. After the bell rang several times at various intervals, I asked the nurse what the sound meant. She said if that particular monitor's bell went off it meant the patient was not getting sufficient air in her lungs and couldn't breathe. The blood pressure monitor was self explanatory. Currently its numbers were a bit high.

The third monitor was for her heart. Of course, I inquired about that monitor too. Those numbers were continually changing up and down. She explained that when the patient's heart beats reached 150 it would trigger an alarm at the nurse's station. Did this mean a heart attack was a strong possibility? Allison's numbers often fluctuated up to and past 150 at which point the screen would go blank.

When that happened, a medical professional would immediately come to check on her and reset the monitor.

Upon first arriving and checking out the cubicle equipment, I remember jokingly asking Allison where the heart paddles were. I teased that if she was going to have a heart problem to go up so they could bring her numbers down. If her numbers went down, they might have a problem getting them up and she might leave us.

Her friend had been sitting in the cubicle for a long time and looked exhausted. Because I was staying, I suggested she go home and rest. When this friend left, another came to check on the patient. She was so nervous and anxious, I suggested her going home too.

After both of them left the area, Allison appeared quite calm and peaceful. The telephone rang. It was a relative calling to check on her. While they talked, I left to get a cup of tea. On my way back, upon entering the Emergency Room area the Code Blue alert sounded. I knew it was her.

Her emergency room cubicle instantly became a hive of activity. I parted the curtain, walked in and stood in the far lower right corner. It was a perfect spot out of the way of doctors, nurses and technicians rushing in with additional equipment. They began working on her intently. One nurse was hooking her up to the EKG machine, while another was preparing fluid medication. A medic was putting liquid into a needle and another was assisting the Cardiologist as he began administering the paddles.

There were at least six medical staff members working to save her. Glancing at the heart monitor machine I saw that her numbers were now up into the 220's. Allison was on her way to a major heart attack.

All emergency cubicle rooms are small. The entire time I stood in that compacted space watching, no one said anything to me. I didn't think about it at the time while remaining in my corner watching as the medical staff moved around efficiently and professionally doing their best to save her. Once they stabilized her heart, machines were removed and the technicians and nurses went back to their other tasks.

Her Cardiologist remained after the other personnel left. Allison was awake and he was talking with her. He mentioned her heart monitor number was at 120. But, that this was still high. Doctors would prefer the numbers be down to 110. At that point, I entered the conversation saying that 120 was normal for her.

The Cardiologist was quite startled. With a stunned expression on his face he turned to see where I was. At that moment, I realized that he never saw me standing there. In fact none of the medical staff had seen me. Emergency cubicles are small. Now there were six staff members and additional equipment brought in. I stood in a corner close enough to have touched several of the nurses by simply putting out my hand. Had I been visible, I would have been asked to leave. But, standing in that corner next to the EKG machine being monitored by a staff member, I'd been invisible. During the crisis, I silently watched the emergency room personnel's effort to save her. I'm not sure about movement into another dimension, but I must confess it was fascinating to watch the medical staff react to an emergency.

The Cardiologist recommended Allison remain in the hospital for a couple of days. Once her heart, lungs and blood pressure numbers were within a range considered normal she could go home to recuperate.

ICU Hospital Visit

This was Barbara's Home-going Service. I'd known her for over thirty years to be a quiet, unassuming, but very observant individual. She thought I had a gift and would often advise me not to hide my Light. Of course, this advice was ignored. When she was hospitalized following a surgical procedure, I went to see her.

Upon visiting, I asked her if I could hold her hand. She said yes. As I held her hand, the monitors attached would ring indicating a trip switch. A nurse would come in and adjust the machine then leave. This happened several times. In resetting the monitors, no one ever looked my way or said anything to me and of course I didn't speak. When I intuitively felt Barbara would be okay, I left. Later one of her friends mentioned she'd been in a coma in ICU during that time and carefully monitored. Again came the realization I'd been invisible or in another dimension. Although Barbara responded to my presence, no one else saw me enter or remain at her bedside for close to an hour.

TRAFFIC ACCIDENT

At her Transition Ceremony, I was reminded of an incident that occurred several years before. Early one evening while on my way to the bowling alley I was involved in a multiple vehicle accident. It was on a very curvy thoroughfare whose lanes were not overly wide. During evening rush hour, the roadways heading away from center city are packed with cars, vans, SUV's and small trucks.

I was on my way into the city to go bowling. This particular time of the evening, there were few vehicles on my side of the expanse. Besides having several curves at this part of the drive, there are a couple of dips in the slow lane. The two cars in front of me, a small truck in back, as well as myself were all in the passing lane. We had just come through a traffic signal so none of us were going fast.

The other side of the road was jammed with bumper to bumper rush hour traffic. On this portion of the route there exists a two to three foot concrete barrier separating the outgoing lanes from the incoming ones. All of the traffic on the other side of this barrier had stopped for the red light.

Just as vehicles in my lane went around a curve, the leading car began to move over into the slow lane. Suddenly there was a car being driven at an accelerated speed coming from behind us in that same slow lane. Anyone could tell there was no way the speeding car could stop meaning there was no way for it to avoid hitting the car that just moved over into that lane. As if in slow motion, the driver of the accelerated speeding car crashed into the first car spinning it around before careening into a second car directly in front of me. After demolishing those two cars, it went airborne up and over the concrete barrier. The speeding automobile landed on top of cars in both lanes on the other side of the roadway.

Feeling helpless watching all of this happening, I remembered screaming for Guardian Angels to help those people. While yelling, I was looking down and back at the truck that was behind me. There were two crushed cars in front of me, one in each lane. The speeding car was now resting on top of several cars on the other side of the highway. I remember hoping the truck wouldn't rear end me.

This is where things became a bit other worldly. My car went up over the crushed vehicles in front of me and back down onto the

107

roadway. In a state of disbelief and horror, I continued on to my destination.

Upon arriving at the bowling alley, I must have looked shell shocked and in a daze. Barbara instantly came over and asked what was wrong. I told her she wouldn't believe what happened. She told me she would and was aware of many unusual things that take place in our world. After describing the accident, she pointed out one important detail. I'd mentioned looking down and back at the truck behind me. She pointed out that my SUV had risen above and past the destruction and entered another dimension.

I wondered if this was an hallucination until other bowlers came in talking about a terrible collision involving multiple vehicles that had shut down the roadway. Bowlers coming from that direction were detoured. Fortunately, I didn't hear of anyone dying.

From that time on, Barbara was there if I needed someone to listen. She continued to tell me I was gifted and needed to let my light shine. Don't hide it under a bush she would exclaim. Use the gift God gave you.

NEAR MISS SITUATION

Three of us were coming home from spending a weekend with out of town family. My niece was driving her new Honda with my granddaughter asleep in the back and me in the front passenger seat. It had been a peaceful drive and we were almost home. There were several cars behind us at this juncture, but we were in front.

Upon entering a curve going around the roadway, a large black town car came barreling toward us. Now at this particular spot of intersecting traffic, cars coming around the curve from both directions have the right of way and don't have to stop. But, to keep straight a car must halt at the stop sign.

This big black sedan with tinted windows was speeding toward us and I could sense the driver was going straight ahead. There were several cars behind us all driving at the same thirty miles an hour speed as us. But, the curve slows cars down to twenty-five mph.

Watching the car I thought, the driver's not going to be able to stop. It was aimed directly at us. If it hit our compact the crash could kill us. The front of that vehicle was as wide as the side of our

Honda. No way if we were broadsided at the speed that automobile was traveling, that there wouldn't be serious injury or death.

Suddenly, time seemed to stop. The cars behind us and the one speeding toward us seemed to halt or to move in such slow motion they appeared to have stopped. Our car maintained its same speed as before. As we went around the curve, I told my niece not to stop and to continue driving. As soon as we were out of danger, that big black sedan with its tinted windows barreled across the roadway in back of us and in front of all the other drivers. It went straight ahead.

This was an example of time and space becoming relative for us and for all of the other cars involved in this incident. Time slowed almost to a stop for all of the vehicles but ours. As soon as the danger of our being involved in an accident passed, time went back to usual for all of the traffic.

Chapter 23

FEAR

One of the cleverest devices for mind control is fear...the fear of poverty, criticism, ill health, loss of love, old age, and death.

Napoleon Hill.

Claude M. Bristol in his book <u>The Magic of Believing</u> said, *"What you believe yourself to be, you are. What you exhibit outwardly, you are inwardly. You are the product of your own thoughts"*. When you're afraid, it's a sign that you've allowed your mind to control your thoughts.

Fear is an illusion is easy to say; however, at one time or another I would assume all of us have experienced the emotion. It's a part of surviving life here on Planet Earth. Many times it's apprehension of the unknown. But, it can also be a dread of failure or even future success as well. People have anxiety of flying, dying, the dark, of heights, and spiders, etc. It's not the terror that counts, but how we allow it to shape our actions that really matters.

When we're struggling with daunting issues at home or at work, sometimes it helps to take a breather and step back. As an observer instead of a participant, we might see things from a different perspective. This helps remove some of the emotion attached to the situation allowing more clarity.

Besides a psychological reaction, we can have a physical one. When confronted with a frightful situation or trauma, our heart rate accelerates rapidly and blood pressure skyrockets. We may develop indigestion and have stomach issues. A common reaction is to go into the fight, flight or freeze response. Sometimes our survival depends on how we resolve the situation.

I think apprehension is a shadow side of all of us and will appear at various times during life's journey. When it does, it's important to let go of the negativity that accompanies it. Choose love and let distress go. Surrendering the experience to the Divine Source can be assisted by meditating and/or praying.

Fear limits growth and calibrates below 200 according to Dr. Hawkins Scale of Human Consciousness (*See chapter on Calibrations*). It often leads to anxiety and grief. Just believe that the Universe has your back and move ahead.

When feelings of trepidation arise, think what's the worst thing that can happen? Everything could be lost or destroyed. This occurs on a regular basis to people around the world experiencing natural disasters like forest fires, floods, earthquakes, volcanic eruptions, and tornados. You might even suffer a devastating injury. Athletes and military personnel undergo physical therapy and training while being encouraged to accept the lost of an arm or leg or even worst. They heal the affected area as much as possible and attempt to continue on with their lives. And lastly, you could be killed. That simply means your time in Earth School is finished and you're headed back to the heavenly abode.

AMUSEMENT PARK

As teenagers, we often went to amusement parks with our church family groups. My most dreaded ride was the roller coaster. It went up and up in the air to what seemed like an enormous height at a really slow pace only to speed down tilting around curves and scaring the wits out of passengers. After a great deal of teasing and daring, I decided to try it with my friends. The first time I was scared to death. Going up nice and slow in the car was okay. Coming down I shut my eyes and screamed, but survived. So of course it had to be ridden again. What I discovered was by the third or fourth ride it became boring. There was no longer the thrill of being afraid. The ride that seemed dangerous and unending at first, was now exhila-rating and over in a heartbeat.

Mary Balogh in one of her books writes: "...if we face our worst fears and move forward into and through them instead of cowering or running as far away from them as we can, then we will never have to fear anything ever again".

PANIC ATTACK

A different scary situation occurred recently. I woke up from what should have been a peaceful night's sleep feeling nervous and anxious. There was that gut feeling something dreadful was about to happen. Uncertain what was causing the anxiety, I went outside to get the morning paper. There curled up on a rock near my door was a foot long garter snake. I had such panic it was amazing. My heart started beating rapidly and I felt panicky. What caused this fright? Who knows. I immediately retreated back into the house and shut the door.

This began the onset of nightmares. In the middle of the night I'd wake up screaming, filled with horror. Going to bed no longer guaranteed a good night's rest. As a result of a scary dream I experienced rapid palpitations and an inability to go back to sleep. The choice was to lie awake for hours or simply go read a book.

From that first distressing nightmare on, it seemed like every time I went out my side door a snake was visible. They were a variety of colors, red, green, brown and black, Some plain and others with patterns. Sizes ranged from a few inches to a couple of feet. They would be meandering through the grass, crawling from under a rock, or sticking a head up out of a shrub, but always somewhere close. Each time, I called my husband to remove it. He'd simply pick it up and relocate it to another area away from the house.

As a child, our family resided in a neighborhood where there were lots of wild flowers and bushes. Blackberries grew wild and we picked them at will. If we inadvertently startled a snake, we'd run one way and it would slither away. There was no danger involved.

Years ago as we were leaving my son's violin lesson, he spotted a garter snake curled up in the music school's driveway. He asked if he could have it. We took it home and bought a glass tank to hold it. Of course, it got loose and disappeared. This didn't bother me knowing it was probably harmless.

> *To wake up one morning and panic at the thought of seeing one was thought provoking. I began to question myself about this phobia. Why the fear? This terror lasted for a couple of months. Interestingly, there were more serpents around my home than usual. They would be sitting on a bush by the door, sunning on a rock close by, crawling through the mulch surrounding the shrubs, or leaving recently molted skin.*

Life is interesting. Attempting to understand what was happening brought realization that my fear was an illusion. All of the snakes around my property are harmless. My only recourse was to face my alarming fright and let it go. A Course In Miracles says, "Nightmares are terrifying sights and screaming sounds brought from the ego to awareness. Look upon them with love and watch them change to peaceful gardens under open skies." So, just as one morning I woke up in terror of reptiles, the fear vanished.

During the Great Depression Theodore Roosevelt assured the country there was nothing to fear but fear itself. He was right. The United States moved from the economic crisis into a time of peace and financial stability. Instead of cowering or running away, we faced our worst fears and moved forward.

It's not the trepidation, but how we allow it to shape our actions and relationships that truly matters. Accept the worrisome situation, pray on it and trust that all will end for our highest good. Again, it's easier said than done.

Chapter 24

DARK NIGHT OF THE SOUL

*It's a lonely, empty, despairing place, but it seems as if
nearly everyone on a spiritual path goes through it at
some time.*

Echo Bodine

Dark night of the soul is an experience where you sense an absence of light and hope. It can often be a feeling of despair caused by an unexpected event. Generally, it occurs as you progress toward a higher state of consciousness.

Your view of life can change in an instant. Joy can become a thing of the past. The emptiness inside makes you feel completely alone. No one understands why you're feeling depressed and at a loss. This experience is a very personal matter.

The dark night can be a short intense period of a twenty-four hour day or it can last several weeks or months. Even though you go through the motions of your daily life, there's a sense of inadequacy. You're not sure what to do next.

Friends will offer advice, but you're aware it's not the solution. Material possessions can't help. You cry out for assistance and pray for resolution to your situation. Agonizingly, there's still a feeling of helpless loneliness. It's a time of great despair with nowhere to turn.

Struggling to survive, you begin to accept your situation. Upon doing this, you're in effect surrendering to what has happened. A peace begins to enter your being. Acceptance is the key. There's a light at the end of the tunnel. You realize you're not alone. There is a Divine Presence available to all.

With the beginning of the dark night, you could witness a changing point in your consciousness growth and development. A higher sense awakens within as a new day dawns. Words and actions alter as you move from the darkness to the Light. The 'Dark Night of the Soul' is now over. Of course, you can have more than one of these experiences during your journey here on Planet Earth.

As I look at a large part of our country during this time of change from the Age of Pisces to the Age of Aquarius, I wonder if this is the Divine Source's version of a collective Dark Night of the Soul. The fires burning in Western United States, Australia and other countries are devastating. Along with floods and wind storms, massive numbers of people around the world are being deprived of everything. There's nothing that can stop nature's destructive path. Families are losing their homes, their possessions, and even their livelihood. Places of worship, employment and education are either burned to the ground, destroyed by floods, or severely damaged by wind storms.

We are currently experiencing a global pandemic. Covid-19 is deadly, and responsible for millions of illnesses and deaths. It's taking a toll emotionally, spiritually and financially throughout the world. Depression and despair will inevitably follow the feelings of helplessness.

Humans are resilient. Some will rebuild and try to continue with their lives. Others may be unable to imagine a future and consider ending theirs. A time of great decision making is at hand. Inevitably, we come the realization that life goes on as long as one is alive. This acceptance and surrender will lead everyone closer towards the Light.

PANIC MODE

For no apparent reason, a usually normal situation can become a frightening experience inducing panic, filled with an intense fear.

Suddenly, you find yourself gazing at a horrifying sight that produces terror within. It can cause sleepless nights. Memories long forgotten re-emerge. During the day you go about your daily life but at night you can't stop the recall of scary events. You might feel deep pain and remorse as images from the past suddenly become shadows in the darkness.

This is also a time of great inner cleansing. Time to purge your memory banks and send unhappy and unkind thoughts into the air for Universal clearing. An opportunity to seek healing and emotional forgiveness. Once these blockages and obstacles are removed, you're released from the terror. Now you become capable of greater humility, trust and understanding.

MY DARK NIGHT

My bout with this type of terror occurred recently. I'd been going about life in my usual relaxed state of being. Suddenly, I began to have nightmares containing serpents. It made me wonder why. Thus began my internal search to discover the reason I panicked. Was this my Universe Initiation test to conquer fear?

The more I thought about it, the more convinced I was of the need to move past this experience. It took several months of seeing all kinds of reptiles every time I went outdoors to achieve this break-through. My acceptance of seeing them and surrendering to the fact I was being tested removed the fear. The nightmares ended and I rarely saw snakes.

Detachment comes with the release of fear and panic. You see people, events and things with greater calm and clarity. It frees you to view the world and events in a different light. You become non judgmental. Again, acceptance and surrender are the keys to releasing one's self from the dark night.

Chapter 25

Spiritual Entities

A form of energy that could be an angel, guide, spirit or lost soul.

Wikipedia

From a very young age, I've had a thing about mirrors and wouldn't look in one if possible. For years, I couldn't explain this reluctance. After a few sessions of childhood memory recalls, I instantly realized why. As a young girl, one day when I looked in the mirror there was another figure standing behind me. But, when I turned around no one was there. It scared me so much that I hesitated to look in a mirror because I wasn't sure what I'd see.

Over the years, there have been occasions when I glimpsed a shadow that quickly disappeared when I turned. Periodically, I felt as if someone were close by, but not visible to the naked eye. We've all probably seen animals sit up and stare at an area of the room as if seeing something or someone. As a child, when elders were asked about these incidences, they said it was probably the essence of a deceased relative or pet animal.

I'm aware now that what I saw or felt as that frightened youngster might have been my spiritual guide, mentor or guardian angel. It could have been here to offer assistance and advice. I needed to learn more about entities. I can accept help from the spiritual realm, but my preference is mental telepathy or a street angel in human form as opposed to an apparition that just pops up.

The vision in the mirror that morning might also have been a lost soul. Entities will try to contact the living. Spirits may have remained in the Earthly realm after the death of the body for a variety of reasons. It could be unfinished business or confusion. If the death was sudden, the body might not know it's dead. It might also be here to help soothe a loved one who is in trouble; or perhaps to accompany a dying person in his/her transition to the other side.

I've learned that if you don't want to have an entity around, it can be told to leave. If the energy seems reluctant to do so, just tell it to go to the Light. This worked fine until the day I realized that I might be the Light. That meant in essence telling the being to stay with me. Now if I feel an unseen presence I tell it to go to God.

HOSPICE SPIRIT

I became more aware of entities when I volunteered at a Hospice. One case in particular involved a client I visited once a week. She was a wonderful lady who lived alone. Her husband died a couple of years before and none of her children lived nearby. Listening to her reminiscence about her family and faith community was always so pleasant. Playing games was especially enjoyable so I'd bring a different one each visit. We usually played for pennies from the games jar. Of course, she always won, delighting her to no end.

> She had to be hospitalized as time for her departure from life here on Earth neared. During my final visit I stood at her bedside for a short time watching her sleeping peacefully. Knowing this was my final opportunity to chat, I said what a blessing it had been to visit with her. Then I recited a couple of prayers for her peaceful transition.
>
> As I said goodbye and was turning to leave, a coolness hovered near my ankles. It followed me out of her room and down the hall toward the elevator. I was surprised at feeling this energy, but quite aware of it. This had never happened before so I wasn't sure how to handle the situation and I certainly didn't want it to follow me home. At the elevator, I mentally told the energy to go back. The lady needed to be able to transition quickly and would need its' help.

It continued to hover around my ankles. I felt the presence leave upon entering the elevator. As I went to the garage to get into my car, I wondered if that was the lady's soul saying goodbye.

THANK YOU VISIT

Another spirit visit occurred in the evening after helping Laura do a Forgiveness Exercise for her deceased friend. I was relaxing in my den reading when a cool wispy breeze nestled on my left shoulder. It felt like someone was gently caressing me with a hug. The feeling only lasted for a couple of seconds.

I wondered who the visitor was. I didn't associate it with the Forgiveness done earlier that day until Laura called the next morning. She said her friend had come to visit in dream form. He wanted to let her know he was at peace and going toward the Light.

I've found that when I ask the Universe a question, it will eventually give me the answer. Of course, sometimes I don't comprehend it right away. When I thought about the visitor, I was given the impression Laura's friend was thanking me for my intervention on his behalf.

ENCASEMENT EVENT

Most evenings during meditation, I assume my usual kneeling position and set a timer. This particular evening, it was set for thirty minutes. Midway into the meditation I suddenly felt a very cold energy. It began at my feet and rose slowly wrapping itself around my entire body as it proceeded upward toward my head. The pressure felt like being bear hugged. I was being enclosed within a cold bubble.

I wasn't sure what was happening. This was a new experience. When something transpires beyond my understanding, I go to God in prayer. Remaining in my meditative position, and assuming an inner peace, I began repeating the Lord's Prayer, the 23rd Psalm and the Hail Mary over and over. Although this was an unforeseen situation, I consciously knew to remain calm. The coldness continued upward movement enveloping my body. As it approached my shoulders, a warm peaceful energy began entering my crown area. Warmth methodically flowed downward from the top of my head. The cold energy ceased movement. The warm energy slowly and steadily moved the cold energy down my body and off my feet. It left and my body was encased in a peaceful warmth from above.

This episode occurred slowly during a fifteen minute time period. I thanked the Holy Angels for protecting me and continued with my meditation. Normally the entity presence will feel like a cool gentle breeze that comes and goes in a wispy sensation. This was a really cold energy that attempted to encase my entire body. I don't know who it was or why it came, but it hasn't happened again. I truly appreciated the wonderful power of Prayer.

I sent an email to Bill, someone I consider a friend and mentor about this incident. He said we are surrounded by entities all of the time and suggested that if I saw or felt them I should ask their name. They have to either tell me who they are or disappear. My problem with this approach is how do I hear them if they tell me. I've also been told to simply tell them I will not accept them and send them to the Light. However, if your body vibrates at a high level, you might be the Light.

CONTACT ALERTS

One of the ways entities show they're near is by electronic interference. My lamp light will flicker, or my telephone will ring once or twice and no one is there. My computer screen will activate even though it's turned off. When this happens, I wonder who is trying to get my attention and why. Sometimes, I'll get a thought of someone it could possibly be. Eventually Divine Source will let me know who the contact is and why it came.

I think of most entities as spirits adrift here on Earth. Souls that haven't gone to the other side for one reason or another. In the case of Laura's friend, he needed to have her forgiveness to release him. Victims of sudden death by accident, suicide or murder can also linger. They might not realize they've died or know where to go. Now, whenever I detect an entity, I tell it to go to God or to Divine Source.

In the beginning my experiences were mostly an awareness of an unseen presence. It made me nervous to feel their energy. Now, when I see shadows, experience electronic incidents or feel a cool light breeze it no longer bothers me. The cold encasement attempt was the exception. I'm still not sure what that incident was about.

SAYING GOODBYE

Sometimes even after the person has left their physical framework, they still cannot leave this third dimension. Loved ones refuse to let them go. This means they'll stay nearby allowing loved ones the comfort of their presence. However, it also puts the spirit in limbo in our world. The soul connection is so strong the spirit will stay until it's given permission by a loved one to leave. The choice for loved ones is to keep the spirit wandering or to let him/her go to be with God.

ENTITY CLEARING

Smudging is a method used if the atmosphere within my home feels heavy and stagnant. This is a way of removing unwanted energy.

There are many reasons you might need to clear the air in your living quarters. A new home or apartment might still have energy left by the previous owners. Or, you might have had a devastating event occur in your life such as divorce or death of a loved one. Going about our daily lives, we encounter energetic auras around everyone we meet. Sometimes this energy attaches itself to us and we take it home. Smudging can assist in clearing the environment.

The first time I smudged I was kind of reluctant, not quite knowing what to expect. I purchased the white sage bundle and waited until I was the only one in the house. There would be an herbal aroma and I wasn't sure how to explain what I was doing if anyone asked.

The entire process took about 15 minutes. When completed, as I moved around the rooms, I could feel the difference. The air felt lighter and more peaceful. Now smudging is done whenever I feel it's called for. The technique listed in the Appendix is the one I use.

SALT BATHS OR SHOWERS

Smudging will clear our home but sometimes we need to clear our body. As we go through our daily lives, we come into contact with all sorts of people. Their energies can vary from positive to negative depending on what's occurring in their lives.

Teachers come into contact with students from various walks of life, some living in abusive situations. Medical staff deal with life and death events on a daily basis. Patient conditions dictate their energetic composition. Sales personnel also come into contact with people constantly in their line of business. Some are satisfied with results and others quite displeased.

Walking down the street, in an elevator, on an airplane, or in an Uber, we come into contact with other people's energy. Sometimes, that force will attach itself to us and we take it home. This is especially true if children or pets are involved and our emotional attachment comes into play.

When you have an accumulation of these attachments, your body will often feel sluggish, tired or drained. One method of removing the energy of others is to take an Epsom salt bath. Fill the bath tub with reasonably warm to hot water, add a half cup of Epsom salt and a dash or two of bubble bath. After soaking for at least fifteen minutes, when getting out of the bathtub your body will feel lighter and relaxed. There are many other types of salts that can used such as Lavender bath salt, etc.

If it's not convenient to take a bath, you can take a salt shower. Simply wet your entire body in the shower. Take a handful of your favorite bath salt and rub it from your throat down your torso. Let it stay on for a minute or two and then wash it off.

Chapter 26

THE WATCHER

I'm not sure when a phenomena affectionally called the Watcher first appeared. It was many many years ago. I call him my Watcher even though his gender and species is unknown. The only thing visualized, like the view from a microscope, is a single Eye. Never two of them, just the one.

The iris is usually a caramel shade of brown, with the centered pupil being a deeper or darker brown or black. It's surrounded by white with a thin black outer border. I don't recall noticing eyelashes and can't tell what body framework or structure is attached. It goes without saying whomever the eye belongs to must be quite large.

Size can vary from an inch to close to five or more, depending upon where it appears. If seen on a human being, it will try to blend close to the size of the person's eye. But when it shows up on a wall or a painting, it can materialize quite large.

It becomes visible to me at various times, simply arriving out of nowhere. I've seen it in the morning, afternoon and evening. There's no set time, place or pattern for it's visit. With my aging, considerable thought was given to finding out what this viewing was about. I sought information on the internet. Imagine my astonishment upon seeing the Eye of Horus, an ancient Egyptian symbol of protection. The similarity was amazing. It mentioned the symbol was also displayed on our U.S. currency. Funny how we use money all of the time without really paying attention to what is inscribed on it. George Washington our first President, is on the front of the one dollar bill. The Eye of Horus is displayed in the top portion of a pyramid engraved on the back. This was a description of my Watcher.

Watcher's Appearances

On one occasion while visiting my son, the Eye appeared on his forehead. It suddenly materialized on his face like a mysterious third eye. At the time, we were discussing a position he was thinking of applying for.

It emerged on one of my husband eyes at home. Interestingly, I wondered what thoughts were going through his head at the time. There was such a pensive expression on his face. In this instance, it appeared directly on one of his eyes as opposed to another area. But it was obvious because it moved independently from the other one.

One evening while studying for my Ministry School exam, I could feel someone watching me. Looking up from the papers and scanning the room, there was an enlarged Eye appearing over a third of a painting hanging on the wall.

My son and I traveled to a home going service for a family member in another state. Because of the lateness, we were staying over at another relative's home that night. It was a warm summer evening. A group of us were sitting outdoors holding conversation about many topics in general and individual issues in particular. As I was speaking to one of the young ladies, the Eye suddenly appeared startling me so much that I froze. It seemed to cover the girl's entire face. My son noticed my reaction and later questioned what caused the rigid response. This young lady was experiencing depression because of feelings of rejection by others and low self esteem. At the time My Watcher appeared, the group of us were trying to help her understand that we are all creations of God and He doesn't make mistakes. We wanted her to accept who she was, relax, and continue to enjoy being currently employed. The point of our discussion was to let her know she was a child of the Divine Source.

In the beginning, when my Watcher appeared, it would cause alarm. Looking back on the many incidences, I realize that at no time did I ever feel threatened. It's just one of those many unusual occurrences that are a part of existence here on Planet Earth in this life time. But it does make one wonder if we are someone's experiment. Is the Watcher looking at specimens through a microscope. It's like being in a laboratory Petri dish. Or, are we the pieces in a Sim City computer game. Another 'Aha' moment!

Chapter 27

CONCLUSION

Several evenings in a row, I've dreamt about packing up to leave and not knowing where to go. My mind was experiencing a sort of restlessness. Not that I was lost to reality, merely being made aware in the dream state that I was seeking something. Have you ever felt like you were incomplete? As if part of you was missing? There was simply a feeling of loss deep within.

My initial thought in my dream state was I'm looking for my home. I didn't know where to move or how to get there. While walking, I became aware of music in the distance. Softly playing one after the other, were the songs Somewhere Over the Rainbow, then Amazing Grace, followed by an old Broadway show tune, Get Me to the Church on Time. These melodies repeated over and over again in my head while traveling along the quiet peaceful road.

Eventually, I encountered a group of young people of diverse ages, racial ethnicities and genders. They started toward me and then stopped. One of the young men said, "We can't touch her. She's not one of ours. She's His!" While still gazing at me they slowly walked pass, continuing on their way. I haven't the slightest idea what this short interval meant. But I've thought about it often. Who were the young people and what did they mean by the statement "She's His!"

A short amount of time later on the path, there suddenly appeared a tall handsome young African gentleman. He was attired in an exquisite kente cloth outfit designed of gold and yellow with matching headband. I could see everything about him but his facial features. They were a bit obscured. Although he was a stranger and unknown, a sense of peace exuding from his presence surrounded me.

Upon awakening, conversation from the young group kept reverberating through my mind. I am His they said. We can't touch her, she's not ours. And the African gentleman–was he an Archangel? He exuded an aura of peace and tranquility. Words from the New Testament came to mind, "Seek and Ye shall find". The question is who or what am I seeking and how would I know when I find it?

Life at the time was monotonous. Every day activities were routinely performed. It's as if I was in limbo. Ahead was a fork in the road. Should things stop at this juncture or continue to move forward, that becomes the question?

Currently I'm in the process of perusing <u>The Master Answers</u> by Maharaj Charon Singh. For a while now I've put off finishing it. In the past this has happened only twice. Procrastination occurred during the reading of two other particular books: <u>Oneness</u> by Rashi and A <u>Course in Miracles.</u> After much thought and dream contemplation, perhaps my hesitation is because this book, like the other two, has the potential to change my life. Seek and Ye shall find. What am I seeking, the 'Path of the Master'? Who knows. Between birth and death we are on a journey which is full of experiences. Never regret them. Learn from what occurs, accept that which we cannot change and move on. Remember the past, look to the future, but live in the now.

I'd like to close this book with the following Prayer attributed to St. Francis of Assisi.

Lord make us instruments of your peace. Where there is hatred, let us sow love; where there is injury, pardon; where there is discord, union; where there is doubt, faith; where there is despair, hope; where there is darkness, light; where there is sadness, joy. Grant that we may not so much seek to be consoled as to console; to be understood as to understand; to be loved as to love. For it is in giving that we receive; it is in pardoning that we are pardoned; and it is in dying that we are born to eternal life. Amen

Appendices

Appendix A

CUTTING THE ETHERIC CORD

START:

- Find a quiet, peaceful, private place
- Light a candle
- Say a Prayer (*You can say the Our Father, 23rd Psalm, Hail Mary, or just words from your heart.*
- Take three deep breaths and go into a meditative or prayerful mode for several minutes to come to peace within.

HANDS:

- Place your hands in a prayer mode at heart level
- Bow your head and say:
- It is my intention to cut (*name of a person*) cord attachment to me at this time. I ask (*name*) to please forgive me for anything I may have done that caused unhappiness in any way. And I forgive you for anything you might have done to cause me unhappiness.
- I wish (*name*) whose Etheric Cord I am cutting love, peace and happiness. And I ask God to shower (*name*) with His blessings.

PROCEDURE:

- Picture scissors in your hand and cut the cords using a scissor motion all around our body from head to toe. Say *"I am removing (name) cord connection,"* while scissor snipping.
- When finished, take three deep breaths and sit quietly for a couple of minutes.

CLOSING:

- Place your hands at heart level and say a Prayer
- Blow out the candle.
- Bow your head and say Thank You ~ or ~ Namaste

Appendix B

FORGIVENESS EXERCISE FORMAT

Forgiveness Exercise can be used to give forgiveness, to ask for forgiveness or both.

FORGIVENESS HEALING IS:

- Spiritual
- Emotional
- Physical

FOUR ELEMENTS NEEDED

- Fire: candle
- Water: glass or small bowl of water
- Earth: flower or greenery from shrub or tree
- Air: small slip of paper with the person's name on it.

STEPS:

- On a small table place a candle, the water, the greenery, and a piece of paper with the name of the person on it. (Or the situation, if it involves more than one person.)
- Before you begin to speak, light the candle. Hold your hands in prayer mode over your heart and say a prayer. *(You can say the Our Father, 23rd Psalm, Hail Mary, or just words from your heart.)*

- Unclasp your hands and just speak to the paper with the name on it. Say everything you need to say to relieve your soul and to clear your mind. Hold nothing back. The water will absorb everything you say.

WHEN YOU FINISH SPEAKING:
- Say goodbye to the person*
- Say a prayer again
- Blow out the candle
- Place hands in prayer mode by heart and say Thank you or Namaste
- Burn or shred the paper with the name on it.
- Place the ashes and the greenery on the ground. Pour the water on the ground too.

Forgiveness has been sought and received. A sense of peace and lightness invade your being. Remember forgiving others and asking for forgiveness is for you and not the other person. Many times, that individual had no idea of the effect of their actions.

---

* If the person is deceased, ask the Holy Angels to take the spirit of (name) to the Light.

Appendix C

A MEDITATION EXERCISE

(10 MINUTES)

Do not meditate within an hour of eating (2 hours if eating a heavy meal).
Meditation slows and calms our bodies.
This could affect the digestive system activities' necessary to process
food intake.

Set a timer for ten minutes. Sit in a chair with your back straight, feet on the floor, head up and eyes focused on a spot in front of you on the floor. Place your hands palm up on your knees or in your lap and close your eyes.

Place your tongue behind your upper teeth. Breathing from your abdomen, take a deep breath. Inhale for the count of four seconds. Hold your breath for the count of four seconds. Exhale to the count of four seconds. Repeat this two more times for a total of three breaths. Inhale through your nose and exhale through your mouth making a circular movement of air.

Breathe naturally now and relax your body. If thoughts come into your mind, accept them and release them into the air. If you find it hard to free your mind of thoughts, use one of the listed meditation method techniques (*Chapter 15*) to relax, breathe softly and quiet your mind.

When the timer chimes, take a moment to breathe slowly before you open your eyes. As you become proficient in meditating for ten minutes, you might want to increase your time until you find your comfort zone.

Optional: This is a way to remove tension from your body before you begin your meditation.

Begin by tightening the muscles in your feet. Now relax them. Tighten the muscles in your legs. Now relax them. Tighten the muscles in your thighs. Relax them. Tighten the muscles in your buttocks. Relax them. Tighten the muscles in your abdomen. Relax them. Tighten the muscles in your hands and fingers. Relax them. Tighten the muscles in your arms. Relax them. Tighten the muscles in our shoulders. Relax them. Tighten the muscles in your neck. Relax them. Tighten the muscle in your face. Relax them. Now tighten all of the muscles in your body from your feet to your head at one time. Relax them. Begin your meditation.

Appendix D

Smudging Technique

INTENTION:

- State your intention to remove any unwanted energy from your residence.

NEED:

- White sage herb
  - You can purchase white sage sticks or bundles at some of the grocery or health food stores.
- Lighter (or matches)
- Container
  - I use a small metal pan with a handle while carrying the herb around. It prevents embers from escaping and is easy to manage.

PROCEDURE:

- Crack a window or door to allow the unwanted energy to escape.
- Place a couple of white sage herb sticks in the pan.
- Light the sticks to produce flames. When the flames occur, blow out the fire. You only want the smoke.

- Carry the pan with the smoking herb throughout your entire
  residence. Use your hand to fan the smoke into every corner
  of each room including hallway, basement, garage, and closets.
  (*Some people use a feather to fan smoke.*)

Should the sticks no longer smoke, re-light them. The goal is to
fan smoke into every corner and ceiling of each area to remove any
unwanted energy.

While walking from room to room, I also say a prayer. This is
optional. You could just repeat your intention as you walk.

- (*You can say the Our Father, 23rd Psalm, Hail Mary, or just words
  from your heart.*)

Appendix E

LAWS OF THE UNIVERSE

Universal Laws are truth. They apply to everyone, governing all planes of existence.

Surrendering to the Laws brings peace and harmony.

Law of Divine Oneness: Everything in our world is connected to everything else. Everything we say, do, think, and believe affects others and the Universe around us. Everything we do has a ripple effect impacting all.

Law of Vibration: All things vibrate and travel in circular patterns. No two things are identical because each has its own vibrational pattern. All of our thoughts and emotions send out vibrations to the Universe.

Law of Action: Make a commitment and engage in activities that support your dreams, emotions, words, and actions.

Law of Correspondence: It holds Oneness together; it is the cosmic glue that connects the physical, mental, and spiritual planes.

Law of Cause and Effect: Relates to our freedom of choice dealing with events. Nothing happens by chance or outside the Universe Laws. Every cause has an effect and every effect has a cause. (Also known as Law of Karma.)

Law of Compensation: For everything given, there will be a return. When given freely from the heart, the gift is returned tenfold. (It's an extension of the Law of Cause and Effect.)

Law of Attraction: We create or attract by virtue of our thoughts, feelings, words and actions, things, events, and people who come into our lives. Energies attract like energies.

Law of Transmutation of Energy: Gives meaning to Free Will. We have the power to choose the directions of our lives. Good thoughts produce good actions and bad thoughts will produce bad actions. Even the smallest action can have a profound effect.

Law of Relativity: Everything in life is relative. Nothing and no one is inherently good or bad. We choose to assign meaning to things.

Law of Polarity: Everything has an opposite. One cannot exist without the other; if there is love there will also be hate, good versus evil, abundance or poverty, etc.

Law of Perpetual Motion: All is energy and energy moves in circular fashion. There is constant movement at all times. Everything has a natural order.

Law of Giving and Receiving: The energies of giving and receiving operate within all of us. To create flow, they need to be in balance.

Law of Rhythm: Every thing vibrates or responds to a certain rhythm. It establishes seasons, patterns, and stages of development. Many cycles in our lives and nature occur in multiples of seven. We will experience positive cycles and negative ones.

Law of Gender: This deals with the two activities needed to create or produce, "Yin and Yang". These functions are complimentary and found on all planes, physical, mental, and spiritual. When we balance masculine and feminine energies, we align with our higher selves in thoughts, emotions, words, and actions.

More information on Universal Laws can be found in:
Light Shall Set You Free, by Norma Milanovich & Shirley McCune
Internet: Nova Lee Wilder, numerologist

About the Author

REVEREND NELLIE JOHNSON, B.S., M.S.

EDUCATOR AND USUI REIKI MASTER TEACHER

I have always known my mother was exceptionally gifted. For the first time, she publicly shares moments of her surreal spiritual journey guided by angels and messengers of God. It's true that every human being has gifts but, not everyone recognizes their unique-ness. In becoming an author, she shares how she came to embrace her loving gifts and, to bridge two worlds in one lifetime along her remarkable sojourn to Oneness.

She taught me there is no judgement of others. That my own bright spots and pain points happen for a reason. That how you react guides your energy field as the co-creator of your circumstances.

What amazes her most is life's repeated patterns, and the ebb and flow with how it all unfolds.

Looking back, she appreciates that she always learned what she needed to know before she needed to know it. And, she always had what she needed when she needed it.

Her love, respect and appreciation for humanity and nature vibrate deeply through her writing. Drawing on more than thirty-five years as an educator, Non-denominational Minister, Usui Reiki Master, spirit guide and also her own personal awakening experiences, she serves as a loving lodestar to many.

It was family, friends, and those who appreciate her gifts most, that inspired this book - and we are forever grateful.

CPSIA information can be obtained
at www.ICGtesting.com
Printed in the USA
LVHW051120030322
712397LV00011B/969

9 781644 505557